Insider's
Kuala Lumpur

Lam Seng Fatt

TIMES BOOKS INTERNATIONAL
Singapore • Kuala Lumpur

C000040229

In the same series

Singapore

Tokyo

© 2000 Times Media Private Limited

Front cover photo: Bes Stock

Photos by Lam Seng Fatt

Published by Times Editions
An imprint of **Times Media Private Limited**
A member of the Times Publishing Group
Times Centre
1 New Industrial Road
Singapore 536196
Tel: (65) 2848844   Fax: (65) 2854871
E-mail: te@corp.tpl.com.sg
Online bookstore:
http://www.timesone.com.sg/te

Times Subang
Lot 46, Subang Hi-Tech Industrial Park
Batu Tiga
40000 Shah Alam
Selangor Darul Ehsan
Malaysia
Tel & Fax: (603) 7363517
E-mail: cchong@tpg.com.my

Printed in Malaysia

ISBN 981 204 876 6

This book is dedicated to my wife,
Patsy Kam, and our son,
Ryan Lam Tien Yue.

Contents

Preface

When I started writing this book, I thought it would be a breeze. After all, I was born and bred in Kuala Lumpur and I had written several articles about the city before.

Problems arose when I started researching the pieces. Writing an impression piece about Kuala Lumpur is very different from writing a historical piece. The latter deals with facts and figures while the former, opinions and abstractions.

Thankfully, the New Straits Times Resource Centre had newspaper cuttings from the early part of the 20th century, an electronic archival system called Library On-Line (LOL) featuring stories from 1991, books, magazines and all sorts of publications. However, despite it being an excellent source of information, there were still gaps to be filled.

My search for further information inevitably led to earlier writers like Gullick and Middlebrook. I had in my collection J.M. Gullick's *Kuala Lumpur 1880-1895*, *A City in the Making* and *The Story of Kuala Lumpur 1857-1939*, which proved invaluable.

Somewhere in a dusty corner of my library, I found a copy of *Malay Sketches* by Sir Frank Swettenham which had greatly influenced Gullick and other writers.

Though Yap Ah Loy was hailed as the founder of Kuala Lumpur, little information about him could be found in newspaper clippings, and much of that was inaccurate. However, after some difficult searching, I located some information on him from S. M. Middlebrook and J. M. Gullick's book *Yap Ah Loy* in University Malaya's well-stocked shop. It was also here where I found another rarity — Isabella Bird's *The Golden Chersonese*.

After completing the manuscript, I bought a copy of H.S. Barlow's *Swettenham*, a newly-published well-researched book that revealed a different, darker facet of Swettenham. After flipping through all 730 pages of the book, it was necessary to amend several of my essays.

I would like to thank New Straits Times Press Berhad's (NSTP) former Managing Director Mohd Noor Mutalib, NSTP Chief Operating Officer Faiz Ishak and my immediate boss Putri Zanina Megat Zainuddin for giving me the green light to write this book. Thanks also to former NSTP Group General Manager of Research and Corporate Communications P.C. Shivadas for permitting me to use the NSTP Resource Centre and LOL services. To the helpful staff of the Resource Centre, thank you.

I must also express my gratitude to Times Editions' commissioning editor in Malaysia Christine Chong, Times Editions' editor in Singapore Tan Jin Hock (for his patience), Dora Yip who took over the book project from Jin Hock, my former boss Philip Mathews for his faith in me (I am not sure whether I disappointed him), former *Sunday Mail* editor Sheila Rahman for her encouragement, and my wife Patsy Kam for being there.

Kuala Lumpur at the start of the 21st century is a city in transition. The greatest building boom in the history of Malaysia, halted by the financial crisis of mid-1997, has changed the skyline drastically. Several mega projects have been completed including the new administrative capital called Putrajaya about an hour's drive from Kuala Lumpur. Even though Kuala Lumpur is no longer the seat of government, it remains its commercial and financial centre. Decisions will be made in Putrajaya, but the wheeling and dealing—and the partying—will take place in Kuala Lumpur.

> *"The city itself was pure, transparent gold, like glass. The wall was made of jasper, and was built on twelve layers of foundation stones inlaid with gems...."*
> *Revelation 21:18-19*

Lam Seng Fatt

The City Centre

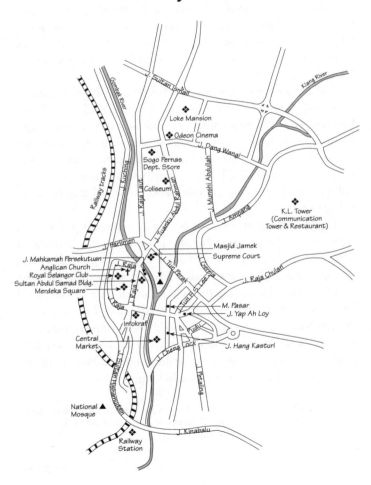

Where Rivers Meet

Confluence of Klang and Gombak Rivers

Was it a Yap or an Abdullah who founded KL?

I t is all a question of political correctness.

Who exactly founded Kuala Lumpur, that little confluence of mud?

Was it Yap Ah Loy or Raja Abdullah? To be specific, was it a Chinese or a Malay?

In Malaysia, such questions regarding ethnicity are touchy even though the authorities constantly discuss issues of race and identity.

In official forms and documents, the applicant is still asked to tick where applicable whether he or she is Malay, Chinese, Indian or Lain-lain (Others). The last category covers Eurasians, Portuguese, and those of Chinese-Indian parentage amongst others. Bumiputeras, or indigenous peoples (including Malays and some native groups from Sabah and Sarawak), still enjoy special privileges in many areas.

One would have thought that more than a century after its founding, the question of who founded Kuala Lumpur would have been put to rest. Alas, it seems to be one subject that is prickly and evergreen, getting resurrected every now and then.

A letter by Don Faust, a reader of the *New Straits Times*, raised the question again on 18 May 1995.

Mr Faust was a mathematician, not a historian, as he candidly admitted, and had lived in Malaysia for eight of the last 26 years.

'With this letter, I hope to encourage public discussion about the history of Kuala Lumpur, to lift the public understanding of its history beyond the level which often cites Yap Ah Loy as the founder of Kuala Lumpur,' he wrote.

Traders and Extractors

He cited three sources of KL's history—J.M. Gullick's article 'The Growth of Kuala Lumpur and of the Malay Community in Selangor before 1880', J.M. Gullick's *Old Kuala Lumpur*, and S.M. Middlebrook and Gullick's *Yap Ah Loy*.

He argued that 'documents show that for hundreds of years before 1800, this particular area with its confluence of rivers providing lines of communication between the straight coast around Klang and otherwise inaccessible inland regions extending right into the Pahang watershed was populated, however sparsely, with traders and extractors of a wide variety of natural resources'.

By the early 1800s, and probably long before that, alluvial tin ore deposits were worked. After all, the rulers in Klang got their income from taxing the boatloads of tin which passed through the town.

Mr Faust said that Kuala Lumpur was both a trading post and transfer station for tin and was peopled by various groups such as Sumatrans, Bugis and others from the Malay archipelago.

By the 1820s, there were already villages at the confluence of the Klang and Gombak rivers (where the lovely Masjid Jamek is located today) and the confluence of the Gombak and Batu rivers. Settlements could also be found at the Batu Caves and near tin mines in the Petaling area.

In 1857, Raja Abdullah Raja Ja'afar decided to make more money from tin. Using mostly imported Chinese labour, he moved upriver from Klang to work the tin fields. Of the 87 Chinese coolies in the first expedition, only 18 survived the ravages of malaria.

The people who over the centuries built their lives around the confluence of the rivers deserve to be credited with the founding of Kuala Lumpur. If one insists upon naming a single founder, it was Raja Abdullah who was the founder of Kuala Lumpur.' Mr Faust rested his case at that.

Indeed, one source says that by 1824, Kuala Lumpur (known as Sungei Lumpur then), was already a trading centre. In the 1840s, tin mining was carried out in the Kancing area and in 1857, mines had opened in the Ampang area. In the 1860s, Sumatrans were working mines in Ulu Klang. By 1859, tin was exported from Kuala Lumpur. Hence, when Yap Ah Loy arrived in Kuala Lumpur in 1862, there was already a settlement which he neither built nor helped to build, let alone found.

The Real Founder of KL

The last time a ruckus was made over the true identity of Kuala Lumpur's founder was in May 1980, when the then Culture, Youth and Sports Minister, Datuk Abdul Samad Idris, suggested that Raja Abdullah should be given that honour. Datuk Lee Kim Sai, the chairman of the Youth wing of the Malaysian Chinese Association, a political party which is a component of the ruling National Front, quickly protested that the statement was a denial of Chinese contribution to the early days of nation building.

One reader responded by arguing that the title of 'Founder of Kuala Lumpur' should in fact go to a person by the name of Hiu Siew whom almost everybody had discarded into the dustbin of history.

It happened that a Sumatran trader by the name of Sutan Puasa had set up shop in the Ampang area where tin was being mined. Sutan Puasa, who was headman of his community, sent word to his friend, Hiu Siew, about business opportunities upriver. Hiu Siew and his sidekick Ah Sze (called Si Keledek, which means 'Sweet Potato', by his Malay friends) went upriver and set up a trading post selling sundry items at the confluence of the Gombak and Klang rivers. His shop was somewhere near where Cross Street (now called Jalan Silang) was and there was a track from the shop to the river bank.

Some time in 1859, Hiu Siew became the headman of Kuala Lumpur, effectively the first Kapitan Cina (literally 'Chinese

Captain', or 'headman of the Chinese community') . Thus Hiu Siew should be given the honour of having founded Kuala Lumpur.

Whatever the case may be, most pundits neglect the very important point that Yap Ah Loy was the third Kapitan Cina of Kuala Lumpur. He succeeded Liu Ngim Kong after serving as his able assistant for six years. The 'coronation' took place in 1868 when Yap was aged only 31.

Why is it then that Hiu Siew and Liu Ngim Kong are uncelebrated? Historians have yet to answer that question.

When Yap Ah Loy was made Kapitan Cina, it was 11 years after Raja Abdullah had made expeditions to open new mines. Although Raja Abdullah was credited with having built a jetty at the confluence of the Gombak and Klang rivers, history did not credit him with building or founding the town.

Obviously, the *New Straits Times* reader Mr Faust, amateur historian but professional mathematician, had gotten his facts, and figures, right.

Bruce Lee of His Time

Yap Ah Loy was a domineering character. Any Kapitan Cina worth his salt had to be, given the wayward behaviour of the gangs of Chinese immigrants who had journeyed to these parts to seek their fortune. Fisticuffs and fights with knives, swords, pipes, and wooden poles were common and Yap Ah Loy was the greatest fighter of them all—the Bruce Lee of his time.

Though it was never recorded whether he was trained in the Shaolin school of martial arts, it is written that he was strong like a bull and had a fiery temper.

An account from Chinese sources said: 'He was not very big or tall but when he spoke his voice was sonorous. His temper was like fire and he had the strength of an elephant. He could support the weight of 100 katis (60 kilogrammes) on his two palms when he stretched his two arms forwards.... On his forehead between his eyebrows was a mark like a Chinese character.'

Gullick wrote: 'A portrait of him shows him to be a short man with a heavy jaw and determined eyes.'

Another account said the scar on his forehead was shaped like the Chinese character for 'man'—a result of a childhood accident. One more account said 'his face had enough determination for an army'.

Another writer pointed out that he was a strong man 'who mastered well the Chinese art of self-defence'.

Gullick added that 'until 1880, he ruled Kuala Lumpur and its surrounding district by the sheer force of his personal authority'.

Sir Frank Swettenham, Assistant Resident at that time, said: 'His perseverance alone, I believe, has kept the Chinese in the country... His energy and enterprise are extraordinary.'

Saint Yap

In his book *Malay Sketches*, Swettenham wrote: 'These Chinese were led by one Ah Loi (sic), a remarkable man, styled the Capitan (sic) China, whose instincts were distinctly warlike and his authority with his countrymen supreme.'

Yap Ah Loy could be quite ruthless, which was to be expected of any *taiko* ('big brother' in Cantonese). During gang wars between the Hai San, who were mostly Hakkas, and the Ghee Hin, who were mostly Cantonese, Yap Ah Loy paid good money for the head of an enemy. Even during war, business was business to him.

Swettenham wrote: 'He offered fifty silver dollars for every enemy's head delivered in the marketplace in front of his house at Kuala Lumpor (sic), and he told me himself that his man who stood there ready to receive the hideous trophies and pay the money did quite a brisk business.'

Fifty dollars for an enemy's head ...

There were stories that when the head of a poor Ghee Hin member was 'served' to him on a platter, he would flick some silver coins to the bearer of good news, after he had examined the head. That proved to be a highly effective way of fighting—and winning—the gang wars.

Yap Ah Loy was not a man to be taken lightly. His extraordinary talents ensured that he was a respected, and more likely feared, leader of the community—a Chinese godfather.

That he became the largest land owner and richest man in Kuala Lumpur in his later years cemented his reputation and made it larger than life. So large in fact, that he became canonised in a very Chinese way.

In 1956, 1,000 members of the Yap clan held a ceremony at the Sin Sze Si Ya Temple, which their patriarch built and is still existing today (behind the Hong Leong building at Jalan Tun H.S. Lee), and declared the senior Yap a saint to be worshipped by devotees.

The narrow entrance of the Sin Sze Si Ya Temple tucked between two buildings.

Three's Company

The entrance to the Sin Sze Si Ya Temple at Jalan Tun H.S. Lee is so narrow, squeezed between Hong Leong building and a row of prewar double-storey shophouses, that only the devotee would know it leads to a temple. The uninformed passer-by would just walk past it without realising the colourful history of the temple that Yap Ah Loy built.

There are three deities there—Sen Ta, Shin Kap and the builder of the temple, Yap Ah Loy himself. Yap Ah Loy was bestowed sainthood by the Yap clan in 1956 and the Kapitan Cina's portrait, next to an urn filled with joss sticks, can be found in a side altar. The temple was originally named after Shin Kap, Kapitan Cina of Sungei Ujong, whom Yap Ah Loy had served under.

He was later deified in Malacca following reports that his spirit could be contacted at his grave through a medium, and that believers had either struck it rich or had their sicknesses cured by him. Devotees built a temple in Malacca in his honour and he had a large following of worshippers, especially from the Hakka community.

An account related how the dead Kapitan Shin Kap appeared to Yap Ah Loy in a dream, telling him that he would help him win the war in Selangor. When reports arose that the deity Sen Ta had possessed mediums at Shin Kap's temple, a link between the two deities developed.

Sen Ta was a mandarin who lived near Canton in China. He was deified after his death and became a popular deity in the southern parts of China. The cult of worshipping Sen Ta (or Sin Sze Si Ya in Mandarin) spread to Malaya through the Chinese coolies who made their way here. The site of the temple in Kuala Lumpur was chosen when a newly arrived coolie, possessed by Sen Ta, revealed that if a temple was built on that spot, believers would receive boundless riches and good fortune.

Yap Ah Loy built that temple to honour the two deities in 1864. At that time, he probably never knew he too would be honoured there some day.

Upward Mobility

Yap Ah Loy had more earthly origins. He was born Yap Tet Loy in Kwangtung, China, on the eighth day of the second moon of Emperor Tao Kong's reign, which corresponded to 14 March 1837. His parents were said to have been from the village of Tam Shui in the Kwai Yap district of the Fui Chiu prefecture. He was a Fui Chiu Hakka. He boarded a junk at Macau and sailed to Malacca, reaching the destination as a penniless immigrant. One source said he left China with only 80 dollars in Chinese currency.

Starting his career as a coolie, he gradually moved upwards in status—first camp cook, then pig dealer and bodyguard, and later assistant to the Kapitan Cina of Kuala Lumpur. Finally, he became Kapitan Cina and Sultan Abdul Samad gave him an official seal and the title Seri Indra Perkasa Wijaya Bakti. That was how upwardly mobile an ambitious young man could be in those days.

Apparently, when he was 'crowned' Kapitan Cina by the Sultan, Yap Ah Loy was taken to the highest elevation of Batu Caves and gongs were beaten throughout the land. Such stories served to cement his reputation as somebody of greatness.

Being a Hai San secret society member, he made his mark in Sungei Ujong.

Gullick's account said that when Yap was 17, a recruiting agent went to his village with glowing tales of wealth to be gained in Malaya and Yap signed up and sailed to Singapore.

Middlebrook said Yap's first job was at a mine at Durian Tunggal, near Malacca town. He then moved on to work for an uncle, Yap Ng, who had a shop in Kesang.

The relationship between the two Yaps, however, did not work out right and the uncle gave Yap Ah Loy about $100 and asked him to return to China. He went by sea from Malacca to Singapore and while waiting for the ship to set sail to China, he gambled and lost all his money. He decided to walk to Lukut, a town in Selangor, where he met up with a cousin, Yap Fook.

At Lukut, he became a camp cook and managed to save some money which he reinvested in rearing pigs, selling the meat in exchange for tin which he in turn sold to dealers. Even then, he was showing signs of his business acumen.

As a pig dealer, he met fellow Fui Chiu Hakka workers at mines in Rasah, near Seremban. Among them were Yap Ah Shak, an influential 'gambling farmer', and Liu Ngim Kong, a *panglima* (lieutenant) of Shin Kap, Kapitan Cina of Sungei Ujong. This meeting was to mark Yap

From pig dealer to Kapitan Cina ...

Ah Loy's meteoric rise to power. Soon after, he became Liu's assistant and head fighter.

Fighting broke out in the tin mines between two groups that sided different Malay chieftains. The group led by Shin Kap was badly beaten and the Kapitan Cina, with a few loyalists, managed to flee into the jungle. Within days, they ran out of food and were forced to seek aid from the Malay settlements. Of all persons, Shin Kap had to bump into the enemy. The Malay chieftain promptly beheaded him.

Legend has it that when his head was chopped off, the blood that flowed was white. Shin Kap was later deified in a temple in Malacca.

The fighting was the beginning of the Sungei Ujong Massacres which lasted six months with a death toll of 4,000 Chinese. In the end, the Malays and Chinese decided that it was far less costly in terms of money and lives to declare peace. They appointed Yap Ah Shak as Kapitan Cina who hung on to power for only a short while before requesting Yap Ah Loy, who was still recovering from a gunshot wound in his thigh, to take over. Thus in a matter of months, Yap Ah Loy had risen from pig dealer to Kapitan Cina.

Bird's Eye View of Ah Loy

Isabella Bird, a lady of the Victorian age who travelled to this part of the world in 1879, wrote in *The Golden Chersonese*:

'Actually the leading man, not only at Kwala Lumpor (sic), but in Selangor, is Ah Loi, a Chinaman! During the disturbances before we 'advised' the State, the Malays burned the town of Kwala Lumpor three times, and he rebuilt it, and, in spite of many disasters stuck to it at the earnest request of the native government. He has made long roads for the purpose of connecting the most important of the tin mines with the town. His countrymen place implicit confidence in him, and Mr Syers, the admirable superintendent of police, tells me that by his influence and exertions he has so successfully secured peace and order in his town and district that during many years not a single serious crime has been committed. He employs on his estate—in mines, brickfields, and plantations—over four thousand men. He has the largest tapioca estate in the country and the best machinery. He has introduced the manufacture of bricks, has provided the sick with an asylum, has been loyal to British interests, has been a most successful administrator in the populous district entrusted to him, and has dispensed justice to the complete satisfaction of his countrymen. While he is the creator of the commercial interests of Selangor, he is a man of large aims and of an enlightened public spirit. Is there no decoration of St. Michael or St. George in reserve for Ah Loi?'

Liu Ngim Kong, in the meantime, had also recovered from his injuries and in 1861 made his way to Kuala Lumpur, apparently at the invitation of the first Kapitan Cina, Hiu Siew.

Liu became Hiu's head *panglima*. When Hiu died less than a year later, Liu ascended the throne and summoned Yap Ah Loy, then Kapitan Cina in Sungei Ujong, to assist him.

At Kuala Lumpur, Yap managed Liu's mines while running two of his own. When Liu died in 1868, Yap became Kapitan Cina of Kuala Lumpur, and the rest is history.

Strangely enough, earlier European historical accounts of Selangor and Kuala Lumpur do not mention Yap Ah Loy even though he was the most important person in the town then.

In 1980, a grandson of Yap Ah Loy related the history of his grandfather in a gathering of fellow Yaps.

His story went that Yap Ah Loy was from a large and poor family. Deciding to go overseas to make his fortune to help his kinsfolk, he came to Malaya in 1854. He went to Sepang (not Kesang) to work for an uncle of his who ran a sundry shop.

One day, he decided to return to China to visit his relatives. His uncle gave him money for the fare and he made his way to Singapore.

Before boarding the ship, he was somehow distracted by a gambling den and he lost all his money. According to the grandson, Yap Ah Loy was so broke that he walked all the way from Singapore to Sepang (not Lukut).

That incident was momentous because of two things—from that day, he swore never to gamble again and he never got to visit his hometown in China after that. Nobody knows why he never visited his homeland in his later days, even though he was the richest man in Kuala Lumpur.

However, as fate would have it, one of Yap Ah Loy's three sons became addicted to gambling and lost the family's fortune.

In 1924, Yap Ah Loy's widow and two sons filed a million dollar petition to the British Resident in Selangor for the refund of money spent by Yap Ah Loy in financing the Selangor Wars, but when told of the legal intricacies and, perhaps more importantly, the costs involved, they dropped the suit.

Yap Ah Loy—The Rebuilder of KL

From 1867 to 1873, Selangor was in turmoil as a bloody civil war raged on for the control of the tin trade.

Yap Ah Loy played a cat and mouse game, displaying fine skills in politics, by first backing Raja Mahdi who controlled the Klang fort, and then Tunku Kudin when he took over

Klang. Even though the fighting was confined to the coastal areas, Kuala Lumpur itself became embroiled in the warring in September 1870. In 1872, after attacks and counterattacks, Yap Ah Loy was driven out of Kuala Lumpur and it was said he made his way through the jungle to reach Klang clad only in a pair of pants.

Early in 1873, a gang of warriors from Pahang, who had been enlisted by Tunku Kudin, invaded Kuala Lumpur and defeated Syed Mashor and his men. When Yap Ah Loy returned to Kuala Lumpur, it was a town in ruins—equipment had been destroyed, sheds burnt and mines flooded. It meant starting all over again and it was his drive and determination that rebuilt the town.

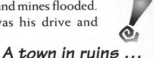

Borrowing money and obtaining lines **_A town in ruins ..._** of credit from the rich Straits Chinese businessmen in Malacca and Singapore, the Selangor Government and the foreign company Guthrie & Co (Guthrie had been a financial backer of Yap Ah Loy and his Fui Chiu Hakka tin miners from as early as 1861), he began putting the town back on its feet.

Tin mines started operating again and the tin revenue just about paid off the creditors. However, the price of tin started to slide and fell to its lowest in 30 years. In 1878, things came to a head when the creditors threatened to recall the loans. Yap Ah Loy's efforts were about to sink like a stone to the depths of a mining pool.

Then, in the words of Gullick, 'luck—miner's luck—saved Yap Ah Loy'.

The price of tin suddenly went up.

From 1878 to 1879, the price of tin doubled. Yap Ah Loy rode this huge wave of fortune, and not only survived the turmoil, but ended up wealthy to boot. At one point, he owned between one and two-thirds of Kuala Lumpur. In 1880, it was reported he owned 64 houses out of the total of 200 in Kuala Lumpur. When the town was laid out anew in the 1880–82 period, he was given 108 lots of land as his property by right of existing occupation, and these amounted to two-thirds of the building land in the town.

He also had a monopoly over the profitable businesses of opium trading, brothels, booze halls and gambling dens. One report said Kuala Lumpur then had 12 opium shops and 225 prostitutes. Another account said he controlled some 300 Chinese women in the brothel quarter between Pudu Road and Petaling Street.

Apart from the sex trade, he had a tapioca plantation, a tapioca flour mill, a smelting shed, numerous tin mines, pigsties, cattle sheds and a quarry. He lived in a large house on the south side of Market Street (now called Lebuh Pasar Besar) where he managed to stash away 12 bags of Mexican silver dollars which went missing after a flood in 1881. The site of the house is now occupied by the Hongkong Bank.

A Minor Emperor

Gullick wrote: 'Yap Ah Loy provided all public services as a personal enterprise—police, prisons, hospital, market, gambling booth and brothels. He kept order, administered justice, maintained a primitive hospital for the sick and supported a large number of dependants. As governor of the town, he was also its tax collector.'

Kuala Lumpur had become Yap Ah Loy's little fiefdom and he, its warlord.

His reign of almost unlimited power lasted till 1880 when the British Resident in Klang, Captain Bloomfield Douglas, shifted upriver and the State Government moved to Kuala Lumpur.

Even the court of the Ching Dynasty in China recognised Yap Ah Loy's status and honoured him by giving him the noble title of Tsoong Yuin Tai Foo.

The epitaph at his grave in the Sungei Besi cemetery in present-day Kuala Lumpur describes him as 'tough, honest, straightforward, just and truthful'.

According to Middlebrook, Yap Ah Loy had suffered from an abscess of the left lung. In March 1885, he seemed to be improving but on 15 April he died. The doctor wrote the cause of death as heart failure or poisoning by fumes (from the charcoal brazier beside Yap), and noted the brightness of his eyes.

In a mark of respect, government offices were closed on the day of the funeral, and the whole town mourned the death of their godfather.

Today, Kuala Lumpur's reputed founder is remembered in the form of a road—Jalan Yap Ah Loy, which is smack in the middle of Chinatown, and measures a mere 80 metres. It is one of the greatest ironies that the once richest and most powerful man in Kuala Lumpur is now remembered by the city's shortest road.

KL's shortest road ...

Life's little ironies—Yap Ah Loy is remembered by the city's shortest road.

Two 'Mad' Salleh Soldiers of Fortune

During the crazy years when, in the words of Sir Frank Swettenham, 'Selangor was so independent in fact that the principal and almost only employment of its inhabitants was fighting', the wars of the Rajas and the Chinese miners over control of the tin trade attracted a motley crowd of outcasts, adventurers and soldiers of fortune.

Not only were there Malays from other parts such as Sumatra and Chinamen out to make a quick killing, but also two Mat Sallehs ('White Men' in Malay). Nobody is quite sure why they ended up in the war as soldiers of fortune. Were they swashbuckling buccaneers—romantic warriors in the Orient in search of the elusive truth? Or were they European riffraff out to make a fortune?

What is known is that they paid their dues dearly.

In *Malay Sketches*, Swettenham said that a few months after his arrival in the East, he was in a Singapore club when he met Cavaliero, an Italian.

'He was quite young, tall, dark, and good-looking, of a pronounced Italian type,' he noted.

He did not know what Cavaliero's occupation was. But he found out later that Cavaliero and a Dutchman called Van Hagen had managed to round up about a hundred people of about half a dozen nationalities and decided to fight for the Viceroy of the Selangor Sultan, Tunku Kudin, brother of the Kedah Sultan who had married the Selangor Sultan's only daughter.

Swettenham wrote that he knew even less of Van Hagen, but had heard stories that he was an officer of the Dutch army and he had been sacked probably for insubordination or indiscipline, 'but he was a man of birth, character and courage'.

Cavaliero and Van Hagen—the handsome, charming Italian and the distinguished-looking Dutchman—in their attempts to rewrite history, ended up merely as footnotes instead.

The duo left Singapore island with their motley group of soldiers and sailed to Klang.

With the help of guides, they hiked 40 kilometres through dense jungle to Kuala Lumpur and reached a hill, said to be Bukit Nanas, near the town where they built a little fort. The enemy surrounded them, harassed them with constant fire, and cut off their supply lines.

Faced with the threat of starvation, the two soldiers and their pack of rowdies decided to take a chance and make their way back to Klang.

The terrain and the jungle defeated them. The story goes that some went off on their own, but the main group led by Cavaliero and Van Hagen somehow got lost in the thick jungle and arrived in a place called Petaling suffering from exhaustion. Apparently, they had walked around in circles and ended up about four miles from where they started. Another story goes that their guide betrayed them by leading them around the jungle before delivering them to the enemy in Petaling.

Petaling was then controlled by a couple of Malay rajas who were aligned to the enemy. Swettenham goes on to describe how the two white adventurers were sent to Kuala Lumpur where they were shot and buried in hastily dug graves.

Swettenham ended his tale thus: 'In excavating for the foundations of the houses which now form the town of Kuala Lumpur, it was usual to dig up a large number of skeletons, the bones of those who had fallen during the years of Selangor's internecine strife... One day, not many years ago, two skeletons were thus discovered. The bones were larger, the figures taller, than those usually met with. They were the skeletons of two men face to face, and locked in each other's arms.'

From Mining Town to Megalopolis

The city centre

What would our pioneers do if they were transported back to the future?

K uala Lumpur's skyline is the result of the biggest building boom ever experienced in Malaysia—lasting from the 1980s to mid-1997, when the economy collapsed because of the devaluation of the ringgit.

If Yap Ah Loy and Raja Abdullah were transported through time to the future, they would be in for a surprise—the tin mining town they lived in has now blossomed into a bustling megalopolis. And there are few natural resources left to work.

The last tin mine in the city closed many years ago and the only reminders of the glorious age of Yap Ah Loy are the numerous disused mining pools dotting the landscape where anglers turn up for some weekend fishing.

Some old tin mines have been filled up and redeveloped into housing estates, while others have been converted into resorts, water theme parks and golf courses.

The Pride of Progress

Malaysians today are rather proud of their capital city. Monumental development projects such as the world's tallest skyscrapers and the world's tallest flagpole have served to boost the confidence of Malaysians who feel that they have made it at last in the global arena. With a skyline which, in their minds, can match Hong Kong's or Manhattan's, they feel they have concrete evidence of their socioeconomic maturity.

But the early settlers of Kuala Lumpur were not so optimistic. In the *Memorandum on the Future Policy of Municipal Schemes in the Town of Kuala Lumpur* written in November 1904 by H.C. Ridges, J.H.M. Robson and E.A.O. Travers (Dr), it was stated that 'it is too late in the day to hope that Kuala Lumpur can ever become a city of great grandeur'. The authors diluted the impact of that statement by adding in the next breath that the city was 'not without its redeeming features'.

Kuala Lumpur then was a far cry from the city today. It was a settlement with 'hovels and huts' along Birch Road, brothels at Petaling Street, handcarts still in use, outdated maps, inadequate water supply, undeveloped lots in Pudoh (now spelt 'Pudu'), narrow roads, insanitary gullies, unlit streets, an inefficient fire prevention system, and forest reserves which were 'used as public latrines and hunting ground for vagrants after a handful of firewood'.

The founders would recognise some things from their pioneering days. The rivers are still around—the Klang and Gombak—even though the meander could have changed and the water is muddier and dirtier with lots more flotsam and jetsam drifting along.

They would also notice something familiar along the banks of the rivers—the makeshift houses of wood. The modern-day squatter settlement would remind them of the old kampungs that were populated by the Sumatrans and some local Malays who had worked the tin mines and other natural resources.

If the founders were to travel further through time to the 21st century they would be in for a shock—they would see buildings built above the very rivers they knew and loved so well.

Another Building Boom

Kuala Lumpur's building boom has fizzled out — the building blocks came tumbling down along with the free-fall in the value of the ringgit and the stock market.

Before the mid-1997 financial crisis, new building projects were launched almost daily.

The Petronas Towers and the KL Tower, the fourth tallest tower in the world, were among those that were built during the recent boom.

Old timers will remember another building boom many decades ago which also changed the skyline of the town.

Back in 1937–38, following the recovery of the world economy from the Depression, there was great optimism in Kuala Lumpur and buildings sprouted all over town.

The Overseas Chinese Banking Corporation built its five-storey building at the junction of Rodger Street and Market Street. The first two floors housed the banking offices and strongroom. The third and fourth floor held offices and the fifth a city club and a roof garden. The unique thing about that building was its basement bicycle park.

The nearby Hong Kong and Shanghai Bank was given a face lift and stripped of its dull 'colonial yellow'. Replacing it was a facade of grey concrete and masonry.

Behind the Selangor Club, the Tin Building, a three-storey office for the Anglo-Oriental (Malaya) Ltd, was taking shape on the site of the Empire Flats which Europeans had occupied years before that. This building, now at Jalan Tangsi, still stands and was at one time the Mahkota College and later, Wisma Ekran.

The leading rubber agency Harrisons, Barker & Co Ltd built its offices resembling a triangle with a rounded apex at Ampang Road. It was the most modern building in town then. In 1937, the Pavilion and Odeon cinemas were also built. The Central Market was also completed around this time.

During that building boom, investors pumped in some $2 million into property development, a mega fortune in those days. Today, that would be barely enough to buy a nice bungalow in Pantai Hills.

Cricks in the Neck

In one of the most ambitious building endeavours yet, the Kuala Lumpur Linear City Project will have retail outlets, condominiums, apartments, offices, hospitals and hotels built above several parts of the Klang and Gombak rivers.

The enormous structures of concrete and steel, like the 88-storey Petronas Towers which became the world's tallest building in 1996, would surely produce cricks in the necks of the pioneers. The closest the founders would have ever gotten to such high structures would probably have been the Batu Caves.

Linear Progression

The futuristic mega-project called the Kuala Lumpur Linear City Project was to be located on the banks and above the very rivers that led to the city's founding.

Despite some muted protests, the Department of Environment approved the Environmental Impact Assessment for the RM5 billion project in August 1996.

However, as a consequence of the currency collapse, the project has been shelved, though the monorail component of the project will still be built.

The Linear City was to be built on a 12-kilometre long corridor which would follow the meander of the Klang river between the bridge at Jalan Tun Razak and the bridge at Jalan Klang Lama. It would have covered 117.6 hectares of river bank and river. A 400-metre stretch of Gombak river near Masjid Jamek was also to have buildings constructed over it.

In exchange for the right to build the futuristic project, the developer Kuala Lumpur Linear City Sdn Bhd, was to deepen and straighten the river and clear its banks of about 1,400 squatter houses and relocate the families in low-cost flats which were to be built in Pantai Dalam.

A component of the Linear City is the RM2.4 billion People-mover Rapid Transit system which is a monorail that will pass through the busy parts of the city not covered by the LRT. The monorail route will start at the Pekeliling bus terminal and end at Kampung Pasir. It will have 21 stations at Jalan Tuanku Abdul Rahman, Jalan Sultan Ismail, Jalan Imbi, Jalan Hang Tuah, Jalan Maharajalela, Brickfields, Kampung Abdullah Hukum and Pantai Dalam.

Work on the monorail is in two phases and construction of Phase One began in October 1996. Phase One was to be an 8-kilometre stretch from Jalan Tun Razak to Brickfields.

This project has stalled though there have been efforts to revive it. All that have been built in mid-1999 are the reinforced concrete pillars to support the tracks. These have been put to good use and now have billboard advertisements especially at heavy-traffic areas like Jalan Sultan Ismail and in front of Sungei Wang Plaza.

Phase Two, which will run parallel to Jalan Klang Lama till the last station at Kampung Pasir, was originally scheduled for completion in 2000 but is far more likely to be ready in the early part of the next century.

Yap Ah Loy and his Chinese cronies would be disappointed that they would have to travel all the way to Genting Highlands to gamble legitimately, and games of chance like roulette and baccarat would not be their cup of tea. Bring back the *sam cheong* (three cards) and the *fan tan* (a card game) at the Old Market Square gambling halls, they would cry.

Those brave pioneers would definitely be confused by the commotion of the city, caused by the thousands of vehicles choking the streets of Kuala Lumpur. If a zooming car missed them, a taxi would not. And if they had roamed Kuala Lumpur before 1997, they would have been assailed by pink minibuses too. The noise of drivers honking and road bullies brawling by the roadside would also have been pretty deafening.

In the old days, the silence of the jungle would have been broken by the rustle of leaves and wings as colourful kingfishers

Already phased out, KL's pink mini buses will be missed by all.

darted across the river. Birds would break into song. The air was fresh and clean and the silence was broken only by confused cockerels still crowing at midday or the woodcutter chopping wood for fuel. In town, it would have been the drunken brawls at the bars, brothels and makeshift casinos. The pace was much slower and nobody complained about high blood pressure or clogged-up arteries. The people got high on opium and not Ecstasy. Nowadays, KL residents complain about the frenetic pace of life in the city and worry about coping with the computerised world of a newly-industrialising nation where the only constant is change and chaos. They read in the newspapers about paradigm shifts and the information age, the multimedia super corridor and other newfangled things that are touted to improve the quality of life. Yet they spend half their time and energy trying to come to terms with these supersonic changes.

Free Mineral Water

The pioneers of Kuala Lumpur would find to their dismay that their currency has little value today. What happened to the beef that used to cost 25 cents per kati (1 kati is about 0.6 kilogrammes), or the chicken eggs that went for 2 cents each, or the whiskey that sold at $1.10 per bottle or the Siamese rice that was priced at $3.60 per pikul (1 pikul is about 60 kilogrammes)? What's this about service tax? You have to pay RM3 for a bottle of water pumped out from a well? And what's mineral water? They had an endless supply of mineral water from the crystal-clear streams up the Klang and Gombak rivers. For free!

RM3 for water ...

In the Beginning

Kuala Lumpur in the 1850s had only two roads—Java Street and Market Street—while the area where Ampang road now is was filled with fish ponds owned by Malay headman, Sutan Puasa.

This was the early Kuala Lumpur that Sumatran pioneer Haji Abdullah Hukum bin Abdul Rahim (1835–1943) recalled in a series of newspaper interviews in 1935. Haji Abdullah Hukum founded a kampung near today's Jalan Bangsar which is named after him.

'The shops then had attap roofs and walls made of woven bamboo strips and the businessmen who were selling things like cloth and food were all Malays who were Rawas and Mendahilings. The community leaders then were Sutan Puasa and Raja Bilah. Both leaders collected tariffs from traders plying the Klang and Gombak rivers. There was also a tax on tin of one ringgit (dollar) per three pikuls.'

Some Chinese reared pigs in the area now known as Pudu Road while there was a small river in the middle of the road now called Jalan Cheng Lock.

In the area now called Setapak (then Hulu Sungei Tapak) and Air Panas (then Hulu Gombak) were padi fields owned by Sutan Puasa.

According to Haji Abdullah Hukum, the Chinese headman then was 'Kapitan Keledek (whose name was Asi) and when he died, he was replaced by Yap Ah Loy'. This is definitely a reference to Ah Tze Keledek, the sidekick of the first Kapitan Cina, Hiu Siew. Historians have yet to clarify this point as other sources say that Yap Ah Loy's predecessor was not Hiu Siew but Liu Ngim Kong and Ah Tze Keledek was never Kapitan Cina.

Concurring with other sources, Haji Abdullah Hukum said Yap Ah Loy owned a gambling hall in Old Market Square and charged no taxes.

After a day in modern Kuala Lumpur, the pioneers would long for home—a Kuala Lumpur of a different time and age.

That Kuala Lumpur had rickety settlements along the banks of the Klang and Gombak rivers. There were no tar roads or overhead bridges, viaducts or LRT tracks, electric commuter trains or sky cranes. And people were growing vegetables where Merdeka Square now is. A network of paths linked the houses of the settlements. People did not die because they were bumped by reckless minibus drivers, but of malaria.

In 1857, Raja Abdullah of Klang and his brother, Raja Jumaat of Lukut, managed to raise $30,000 from two Baba investors in Malacca and sent a group of 87 Chinese tin miners from Pengkalan Batu (now called Klang) upriver in small boats. Gullick described it: 'The boats would carry either 10 men each with a load of provisions or just 30 men without any cargo. For this trip, they were loaded with sacks of rice, jars of coconut oil, with tobacco, spirits and opium in chests. There were hoes, axes and other tools and also baskets for carrying earth. They took weapons for their protection— muskets, gunpowder, knives and spears. Each man had his personal bundle or box containing his spare clothes and his few other possessions.'

At the confluence of the Klang and Gombak rivers, they alighted because the water was too shallow. On foot, they followed a jungle path to Ampang where they began to dig for tin. Ampang is the Malay word for 'dam' and miners had built dams across the river there. Even before these Chinese miners had ventured upriver, there were already Sumatran Malays excavating tin in the upper parts of the Klang river.

A Touch of Magic

Early European tin miners failed where the Chinese succeeded. What was the Chinaman's secret? Was it his much-vaunted business acumen or just plain luck?

It was actually a bit of both—common sense and lots of black magic.

The Europeans had started extensive excavation of earth without conducting soil tests to find out if the land at their mines had veins of tin. The Chinese in the meantime relied on less scientific methods—they hired a Malay *pawang* (a magician of sorts) who had some kind of divining power and could locate tin buried deep underneath the earth. Once tin-bearing land was detected, the Chinese dug to find out just how much ore was there before going fully ahead.

The Europeans, equipped with their steam engines and pumps and well-trained managers, lost out to a group of people who placed their faith in the supernatural rather than the inventions of the Industrial Revolution.

When most of the men were killed by malaria, another group of 150 men went upriver. Some died and they were replaced by other boatloads of workers. More huts were built, and with more miners, there was a need for provisions. Enterprising businessmen went upriver and opened some shops and that was how Kuala Lumpur was born.

Tin ingots were sent to the landing point at the confluence before being shipped downstream to Pengkalan Batu. By 1859, Kuala Lumpur was a bustling exporter of tin. In 1880, it became the state capital and by 1896, it was the federal capital.

Sunset Industry

Popular theory has it that Kuala Lumpur was named after the muddy confluence, but Gullick argues that by Malay usage, it should have been Kuala Berlumpur or Kuala Gombak, because the confluence is where the smaller Gombak river joins the larger Klang. One more theory states that Kuala Lumpur is a corruption of the term Pengkalan Lumpur which means 'muddy jetty'. Another theory has it that Sungei Gombak was called Sungei Lumpur in the old days. Yet one more theory says a tributary called Sungei Lumpur joined Sungei Gombak just before its confluence with the Klang river.

What we know for sure is that Kuala Lumpur began as a small settlement with a population initially comprising mainly Sumatran and Malay adventurers and Chinese miners who lived in wooden houses haphazardly located on river banks and beside the jungle trails.

In the early days, the economic activity and fortunes of Kuala Lumpur depended on tin. A civil war was fought because of the commodity. The fortunes of the town fluctuated along with the fluctuating price of tin. In 1878 Yap Ah Loy, who was struggling to revive the tin mining industry, was said to be on the verge of bankruptcy because the price of tin had fallen. But when the price shot up suddenly the next year, Kuala Lumpur enjoyed a boom and its population increased by 30% that year.

Now, tin is considered a sunset industry and trade in the metal does not even feature in Kuala Lumpur's economy.

Coffee, Tea or *Hevea Brasiliensis*?

Everybody knows that rubber was one of the main pillars of the Malayan economy, but if things had worked out differently, it could have been coffee.

In the late 1870s, European coffee planters in Ceylon planned to leave the island to try their luck in Malaya because a fungal disease had decimated their plantations. In 1878, some of them surveyed Perak and two years later, the Honorable R.B. Downall obtained two concessions totalling 194 acres on a hillock near the heart of Kuala Lumpur which he named Weld Hill estate after the Governor of the Straits Settlements, Sir Frederick Weld. It was the first European estate in Selangor and it cultivated Liberian coffee, pepper and tea. However, Malay small holders were already planting Arabian coffee on the slopes of Bukit Nanas.

Between 1882 and 1883, Downall acquired concessions in other parts of Selangor including a lot near Batu Caves which was planted with Liberian coffee.

Meanwhile T. Heslop Hill, who had earlier ventured into Pulau Ubin and Sungei Ujong, entered into partnership with Ambrose Rathborne and they bought up Downall's interests.

By 1886, Hill and Rathborne had three coffee plantations in the Kuala Lumpur area.

The world prices of coffee beans shot up because there was a reduction in supply from Ceylon and the Selangor coffee planters enjoyed a boom from 1893 onwards. In 1892, there were fewer than a dozen European plantations, but four years later, the number had shot up to 73 and nearly all of them were planting Liberian coffee.

Fungal disease appeared as early as 1894, but it was not fungus that destroyed the coffee industry in Selangor and Kuala Lumpur. According to Gullick, it was due to political events in Europe and South America in the previous decade.

In Brazil, large coffee plantations were badly managed and inefficient and the workers, who were slaves, were freed by a Government decision in 1888. Thus the plantation owners were left high and dry having invested a lot of money with no workers to harvest their product. At the same time, socioeconomic conditions in Italy were worsening. Peasant families emigrated to Brazil where they worked in the coffee plantations and turned them around.

With the increase in world supply of coffee, prices tumbled by the late 1890s.

As the coffee market dipped, the fortunes of the European planters followed suit. But there was another crop which was showing promise at that time. It was called *hevea brasiliensis*, or rubber, as it is more commonly known.

Most of the coffee planters switched to rubber and managed to survive. Some even made fortunes. One coffee planter who invested 4,000 pounds in a coffee estate in Selangor in 1897 replanted it with rubber and within 10 years, his investment was worth 250,000 pounds.

Rubber was cultivated all over the Malayan peninsula and the commodity was a major contributor to the national economy till the era of Prime Minister Datuk Seri Dr Mahathir Mohamad who placed emphasis on manufacturing and industrialisation.

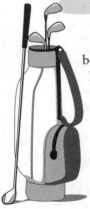

The Sumatrans and Straits Chinese investors have been replaced by the Japanese, Taiwanese, South Koreans, Singaporeans and Americans. No more are the investors armed with parangs and muskets; they now carry credit cards and golf clubs.

Mosque in the Middle

Masjid Jamek
Jalan Tun Perak

Masjid Jamek stands out
amongst concrete towers...

Masjid Jamek—where rivers meet. This is the birthplace of KL.

From the bridge at Lebuh Pasar Besar (formerly called Market Street), one has a good view of the confluence where Kuala Lumpur began as a mining settlement. Today, one can see the domes of the red-brick Masjid Jamek set against the busy modern skyline of a large LRT station, Bank Bumiputra building and other skyscrapers in the background.

A few years ago, one could also see huge pipes snaking their way along and across the river. This ugly feature was criticised by tourists who felt that such a historic vista and photographic opportunity should not be spoilt by such monstrous things. However, history often gives way to development.

Stung by the criticism, the authorities recently relocated the pipes and the picturesque view has been restored.

In the late 19th century, adventurers and miners would row upriver and land somewhere behind today's Citibank and unload their provisions and equipment.

Before the mosque was built, there was a Malay cemetery at the triangular piece of land and an 1889 map showed that the cemetery reached almost to Java Street (renamed Mountbatten Road and now Jalan Tun Perak) and included part of the land where today's Court buildings are.

The map showed that there was a mosque at the junction of Java Street and Ampang Street and another mosque near Malay Street, but these were probably not as significant as the Masjid Jamek.

Masjid Jamek was the first large mosque to be built in Kuala Lumpur. Its foundation stone was laid by the Sultan of Selangor Sultan Sir Alauddin Sulaiman Shah on 23 March 1908. The Sultan returned to Kuala Lumpur to declare the mosque open on 23 December 1909.

It was built at a cost of $32,625 and the designer was Arthur Benison Hubback of the PWD and Survey Department of the Federated Malay States.

National Prayers

Masjid Jamek served its purpose as the main mosque of Kuala Lumpur till the rise in population necessitated a larger one to be built.

The National Mosque near the railway station was built by the PWD in 1965 on a 13-acre site and it included a library, meeting rooms, ceremonial halls and a mausoleum. Its outstanding feature is the 75-metre tall minaret, which has become a unique element of the Kuala Lumpur skyline. Numerous tourism posters, brochures and post cards feature photographs taken from certain angles which portray the onion-shaped domes of the railway station contrasted with the slim and pointed minaret of the National Mosque.

The main dome and minaret of the National Mosque are stylised versions of domes. The main dome looks like a fan-like umbrella.

When the mosque was built, the dome was white. Over the years, it became stained and was recently layered with blue tiles.

Hubback was with the PWD in British India before being sent to Malaya. He also designed the famed railway station and railway administrative headquarters.

Hubback was probably influenced by the Indian-Muslim architectural style that he saw in India and this would explain his exotic works featuring onion-shaped domes and arches of all shapes and sizes.

Crossing the River

In the early 1880s, the only way to cross the Klang river was either by walking precariously on two logs where today's Lebuh Pasar Besar bridge is or by crossing a bridge made of several bamboo poles tied together near the confluence of the Klang and Gombak rivers along Jalan Tun Perak.

In 1880, three years after the British Resident in Klang, Captain Bloomfield Douglas, shifted upriver and the State Government moved to Kuala Lumpur, wooden bridges were built to replace the rickety structures.

The 46-metre wooden bridge at Market Street was in use till 1888, when a 27-metre lattice girder iron bridge was built. This was taken apart in 1901 for a larger steel bridge which remained in use till some years ago, when it was dismantled because it was too narrow to handle the increasingly heavy traffic. A wider bridge of reinforced concrete was built to replace it.

His buildings have become some of Kuala Lumpur's most admired structures.

In 1993, one of the domes of Masjid Jamek collapsed after a spell of rain, but repairs were carried out. The mosque has also been enlarged in harmony with the original style and it remains one of the city's most popular mosques.

Point of Sales

Medan Pasar

Market Square has always been
where the money is.

A conservation success story—Central Market today.

Money has always been the motivating factor at Market Square (now called Medan Pasar). In the past, it was the centre of gambling activities with a casino-cum-market. Miners, hoping to break free from their misery, wagered their meagre salaries in a quick but risky way to make a fortune. Now, it is surrounded by banks and financial institutions. Investment—a more acceptable term for taking calculated risks—has become the great motivator.

Yap Ah Loy lorded over the mining settlement from his house at the junction of Jalan Hang Kasturi (formerly called Rodger Street) and Lebuh Pasar Besar (the Market Street of ancient times) where the Hongkong Bank now stands.

Miners travelling upriver from Klang would disembark at a makeshift jetty somewhere behind Citibank. The miners worked hard and played hard, as was expected of the lifestyle of frontiersmen. That was why Yap Ah Loy set up gambling dens and brothels—to keep his workers occupied and entertained while his own coffer overflowed. The Kapitan Cina earned $250–$300 per month from the market stalls while his profits from the flesh trade are not recorded.

The miners worked hard and played hard ...

The gambling shed was initially beside the river, probably at the row of buildings with Citibank at one end and the Sin Seng Nam coffeeshop at the other. The market was in the middle of a square where the clock tower is today.

Around 1877, Yap Ah Loy's house was described as 'a fairly good looseboard house occupied by the Captain China (sic), the most hospitable of men, and his house was surrounded by attap houses occupied by his coolies'.

Swettenham described the market as 'a very insecure shed' and the den beside the river as 'a huge gambling booth of jungle rollers, roofed with attaps, in which literally all day and all night long, gambling is pursued by a crowd of often excited Chinese and Malays'.

Hornaday, who 'discovered' Batu Caves, was in Kuala Lumpur in 1878 and described the market: 'In the centre of the town is a large market where fruits, vegetables, meats and various abominations of Chinese cookery are sold. The vegetables are sweet potatoes, yams of various kinds, beans, melons, cucumbers, radishes, Chinese cabbage, onions, eggplant and lady's fingers. The fruits were durian, mangosteen, pineapple, banana, and plantain, oranges (of foreign growth), limes, papayah, and other small kinds not known by English names. In the centre of the marketplace are a lot of gambling-tables, which, a little later in the evening, were crowded with Chinamen earnestly engaged in the noble pastime of "fighting the tiger".'

Champagne in Chinatown

It was at Market Square, 'in the largest Chinese store in the place', that Hornaday struck a bonanza—he found Mumm's champagne for sale at 60 cents a quart and India pale ale at 15 cents per pint. He was so pleased with having bought Jules Mumm's champagne at such an unbelievably low price that his only regret was not being able to fill a tub with the champagne and take a bath in it.

From his descriptions, it appeared that the market then looked the same as any wet market in present day Malaysia—colourful, boisterous, smelly and dirty.

Market in the Centre

The most distinguishing features of Central Market are the skylight which runs along the length of the building and the enormous glass-paned windows. In fact, Central Market was Kuala Lumpur's first energy-efficient building—the windows and skylight were glazed with special Caborex rolled plate glass which transmitted only 20% of the sun's heat and 61% of the light.

Central Market was built at a cost of $500,000 in the mid-1930s near the site of the old market. Designed by R.H. Steed of the Town Engineering Department (though the design has sometimes been credited to T.Y. Lee), it had 6,400 square feet of space. It was originally designed with two storeys.

It had 21 gates facing the Embankment and Rodger Street (now called Jalan Hang Kasturi) while the main entrance faced the old McArthur Street. Its frontage measured 58 metres while the depth was 122 metres.

Central Market won the Best Decorated Building award in a competition held in conjunction with the coronation of Queen Elizabeth II in 1953.

It served as Kuala Lumpur's central market until the 1980s when wet markets were opened in suburban areas to reduce traffic congestion in the city centre.

Before the demolition men could turn up, a decision was made to turn it into an arts and crafts centre oriented towards tourism.

It was refurbished and a second-level was added. It reopened on 15 April 1986 with a tenant-mix that included batik printers, Chinese seal makers, portrait artists, glass craftsmen, antique and curio shops and T-shirt artists.

It also had two Indian-Muslim restaurants offering excellent fish head curry and crispy *roti canai.*

There were two pubs with one, the Riverbank, offering some of the 'coolest' jazz music in town. It soon became the watering hole of Kuala Lumpur's yuppie crowd who sat outdoors and sipped wine coolers.

Today, the tenant-mix has evolved—a Chinese brush artist, a Chinese restaurant and lots more shops selling Balinese and Thai craft items. One section has kampung-house facades and the shops sell Malaysian craft items like *wau* (kites), *songket*, silverware and batik.

A section of Jalan Hang Kasturi has been turned into a pedestrian mall, the city's first.

Behind the Central Market, several old shoplots have also been converted to house cineplexes, eateries and boutiques. This project, called Central Square, is interesting because the shops' facades have been retained while the rear portion is in a wildly postmodern architectural style.

A bridge links Central Market to Dayabumi and the General Post Office. The last colonial postbox is located near Central Market's entrance.

Market Square in those days had two streets—Macao Street (the existing sideroad in front of Citibank) and Hokkien Street (now called Medan Pasar). These road names probably reflected the origins and dialect group of the original residents.

The big fire of January 1881 razed the whole of Kuala Lumpur, including Yap Ah Loy's house, the gambling den and market. The town was rebuilt with brick and tiles, but on 21 December that year, there was a major flood and Yap Ah Loy's new house collapsed.

Swettenham had never really liked the market and gambling den at Market Square *Indescribable* (he commented tersely that the 'filth of the *filth ...* market is indescribable') and wanted both removed, claiming that they were on government land. Yap Ah Loy demolished the gambling shed and rebuilt the market with brick pillars and zinc roof and managed to get a lease for the plot of land.

Only after his death in 1885 was the market shifted to a site behind the Kapitan Cina's house, along Rodger Street, near where Central Market now stands. In an 1889 map, the market was already located at Rodger Street.

Yap Ah Loy's descendants wrangled with the government over compensation for the old market—they demanded $9,586.85 while the government offered only $2,500. It is not recorded what the outcome was.

The new market was slightly better than the old market. It was 76 metres long and 27 metres wide and had wooden walls, a tiled floor and a zinc roof. It also had 'ornamental cast-iron railings and gates'. That structure served the needs of the town for almost 40 years before it was decided that a more permanent and larger market made of brick and cement should be built.

The interior of today's Central Market is new and is divided into two levels. The skylight, windows and exterior walls have not been changed.

Central Market was almost demolished when there were plans to bring it down to make way for an office block. It was saved when a proposal to turn it into a tourism-oriented conservation project like Covent Garden in London was accepted by the authorities. The city should be thankful for that, as a historical link to Yap Ah Loy would have been erased forever if it had been demolished.

As it turned out, Central Market became one of the most successful conservation projects of the country.

The Golden Mile

Jalan Tuanku Abdul Rahman

Why hasn't the popularity of the quaint,
old shops faded even in the face of
new shopping malls?

Jalan Tuanku Abdul Rahman, or TAR Road, is one of those historic roads in Kuala Lumpur which has evolved to become an important shopping street. In the old days, the Europeans did their shopping at Market Street, where the city's first department store Chow Kit & Co was located, and later at Java Street where there was a row of shops which included such famous names as Robinson's, John Little and Whiteaways.

However, the glorious days of Market Street and Java Street have faded away.

Jalan Tuanku Abdul Rahman, which was called Batu Road before 1963, started out essentially as an extension of Gombak Road, the road in front of the Sultan Abdul Samad Building now called Jalan Raja. It **Rough road ...** was a rough road that led to tin mines in Batu and Rawang. Later, it was connected to Java Street.

As the condition of the road improved, rows of shops were built at Batu Road, some as early as 1915, somewhat like an extension of Java Street's shophouses. The shophouse at the junction of Java Street and Batu Road was built in 1920.

Traders, the majority of whom were Indians, rented the premises at $30 a month from the landlords who were mostly *chettiars* (Indian moneylenders). Initially, many of the shops were used as warehouses.

A Batu Road address might not have been that sought after by the rich and famous of old Kuala Lumpur, but at least two of the town's luminaries lived there—Loke Yew and Thamboosamy Pillai.

Some of the companies that started operating there have become household names—Globe Silk Store, G.S. Gill, Coliseum, P. Lal Store and P.H. Hendry. Some of them shifted, only to occupy other premises along the same road.

P. Lal Store, famed for selling winter clothing and British-made leather shoes, started out in 1929 at No. 57. It moved a few doors away to No. 49 in 1945 and, recently, moved into its own multistorey modern building called Wisma Lal Doshi at No. 135.

G.S. Gill, which has become synonymous with sports goods and Adidas products, started in 1945 at No. 106 and has occupied the same premises ever since, though the old shop has been replaced by the multistorey Wisma Harwant.

Globe Silk Store opened at Batu Road in 1947. It had been founded in Segamat, Johore, 17 years before by Tirathdas Jethenand. In 1957, it shifted to a four-storey building. Then, it relocated to a refurbished row of old shophouses along the road near Odeon cinema, and has been operating in the modern multistorey building since.

Towering Inferno

Just when Malaysians were thrilled by the movie *Towering Inferno*, the Campbell Shopping Complex caught fire and became Kuala Lumpur's very own fiery drama.

In April 1976, fire broke out in the 20-storey skyscraper and blazed for a few days, destroying 156 shops and 41 offices.

After being left vacant and barricaded for some time, it was repaired at a cost of RM10 million and reopened, but its heyday was over and newer malls nearby like Pertama Complex and Sogo pulled in the shoppers.

Other stores like Kamdar (which took over the old Mun Loong block while Mun Loong has taken over the Hankyu Jaya store in Chow Kit), Sharafali's (established in 1950) and

Selangor Emporium started business there later, but have become famous too. People also remember establishments like Peiping Lace, Chortirmall, Central Shoe, Tivoli Hotel Pub and Restaurant, Rex Hotel, Kowloon Hotel, Tang Ling Shopping Centre, Seng Hup which sells lighting accessories, K.S. Gill which specialises in pens, C. Nang Hong & Co and Kee Huat Radio Company. Batu Road was where A & W, Kuala Lumpur's first fast-food outlet, opened. It was also where Burger King started out and flopped. It has since made a successful comeback in the Malaysian market.

Development has not given the road a miss and several projects have been embarked on. Rows of shophouses have been demolished—with only their facades remaining as required by City Hall's conservation policy—to make way for office blocks, near Bata and the former Selangor Emporium.

About 20 years ago, there were several blocks of low-cost flats diagonally opposite Odeon cinema (which has been turned into a retail centre) called Sulaiman Court. These were demolished and on that site now stands Sogo, the giant Japanese department store.

Three Cents for Coffee

Next to Odeon is one of the oldest Chinese restaurants in the city—Lee Wong Kee Restaurant. It celebrated its 70th anniversary in August 1996. The restaurant, where thousands of couples have held their wedding dinners, started in 1926 at High Street and moved to Batu Road in the 1930s.

Batu Road is also where the old cinema, Coliseum, is. Now famous for screening Hindi movies, it used to stage bangsawan performances in the 1930s and plays like *Hamlet* and *Romeo & Juliet*. When it was built in 1920, it was designed for stage shows rather than movies. Behind it was a bakery which was converted in the early 1920s to Coliseum cafe and hotel.

Old-timers will recall watching *Tarzan* movies at Coliseum and paying 20 to 50 cents for a ticket.

Planters from out of town used to stay at Coliseum hotel and party at the Spotted Dog (their nickname for Selangor Club), a short walk away. They would then return to Coliseum, have a few more drinks at the bar before calling it a night. Coliseum cafe became famous for its steaks and even today, dining there is considered something like a treat. However, although Coliseum's old-world atmosphere is quaint, it cannot match Le Coq D'or at Jalan Ampang.

In the 1930s, Batu Road was a two-way street and traffic was so light that it was possible to park on either side of the road.

Textiles cost 15 cents a yard, ties and socks could be bought for 10 cents, while a mug of coffee cost all of three cents. And the mug was so big that the coffee could be shared by three people.

Much of the area was not developed then and beyond Odeon cinema, in the direction of Chow Kit, there were only coconut plantations and jungle. Even the area between the Gombak river and Coliseum was *belukar* (secondary jungle) and at today's Jalan Masjid India area, beside the Klang river, lay a large tract of wasteland with a few wooden huts.

However, business here picked up in the 1950s and has continued to do well ever since. Even when major shopping complexes opened in other areas such as Bukit Bintang, the glitter of consumer money at TAR Road did not fade. Thus it earned its sobriquet, The Golden Mile.

Poison and *Pondans*

A long time ago, there was a shrine to a poisonous cobra at Gombak Lane, the backlane behind Coliseum at Jalan Tuanku Abdul Rahman.

The shrine was built in 1973 when the owner of a *teh tarik* stall spotted a cobra slithering around. To the Hindus, a cobra has some religious significance and therefore a shrine was built where its nest was believed to be.

Believers claimed that after feeding the cobra with eggs and milk they were cured of their sicknesses. A statue of the cobra with hood open was carved out of stone and placed in the shrine. The shrine became quite popular much to the benefit of the *teh tarik* stall owner.

In September 1981, the shrine was demolished to make way for the multistorey Pernas building. And as is common in such supernatural stories, all sorts of things happened at the work site—cranes and cement mixers mysteriously stopped functioning, a hole caved in twice, and workers fell ill. Apparently, the cobra was angry because it had not been consulted about the demolition of its shrine. City Hall stated that it was an illegal structure which had to make way for progress.

The contractor built another shrine at Jalan Templer, Petaling Jaya, to house the cobra idol (a new one was made) and work proceeded smoothly after that. However, nobody knows for sure what happened to the cobra itself.

Today, most residents of Kuala Lumpur would not remember the cobra or its shrine at Gombak Lane, though some people still frequent the backlane for a very different reason.

Pondans, or transvestites, often move out of their Chow Kit hang-outs to *cari makan* (a Malay phrase literally translated as 'find food' but means 'make a living') at the backlane, attracting a steady stream of people out to worship a different kind of force altogether.

B.P. Doshi, owner of P. Lal, was reported as saying: 'This place has not lost its popularity. When other shopping centres came up, we felt that old shops would be doomed. Instead, there appears to be demand for such shops and the businesses have grown.'

But Batu Road itself was where some of the new shopping centres were built. Near Odeon along Campbell Road (now called Jalan Dang Wangi) is the first modern multistorey shopping mall in the city, Campbell Shopping Complex. In front of Odeon is the Pertama Shopping Complex.

In the old days, any parade in town had to pass through Batu Road. In 1953, there was a Coronation Day parade to celebrate the crowning of Queen Elizabeth II. It was a grand event and the road was jam-packed with spectators jostling each other. The first floors of the shophouses were also filled with people who wanted to have a better view of the colourful and well-lit floats on parade.

In 1967, Malaysia won the Thomas Cup (a prestigious badminton trophy) and a parade was held with the badminton stars sitting in a convertible and waving at the crowds. Later, a celebration dinner took place at Coliseum cafe with the Thomas Cup itself placed at the centre of the table.

National Day parades and the Thaipusam Silver Chariot procession would pass through Jalan Tuanku Abdul Rahman.

Jalan Tuanku Abdul Rahman starts at its junction with Jalan Tun Perak and ends at its junction with Jalan Pahang after passing through the Chow Kit area. In some stretches such as from Campbell shopping complex to Selangor Mansion, even the backlanes are lined with tiny shops.

Every Saturday night from 6 pm to 10 pm, a section of the road from Sogo to its junction with Jalan Tun Perak, is closed to traffic for a *pasar malam* (night market). This night market is colourful, busy and boisterous and simply proves that at TAR Road, shopping has become a way of life.

Shopping Before Sogo

Jalan Mahkamah Persekutuan

Chow Kit was there before the Japanese...

The industrial court building—where entrepreneur Loke Chow Kit opened KL's first department store.

The shops of KL in the old days were rather limited in their stocks. But the Chow Kit emporium (housed in the building now occupied by the Industrial Court) was different.

An 1895 advertisement ran thus: 'Chow Kit & Co, general storekeepers, merchants and commission agents, have always in stock European Goods, Tinned Provisions, Wines, Spirits, Etc. All of the best quality.'

The list of items available was impressive and obviously catered to Europeans—'Fresh pork and other hams and fresh bacons, cheddar, Dutch, Edam and Gouda cheese, Australian butter, Basek's and Heyman's Danish butter, preserved Californian fruits in tins and bottles, Huntley and Palmer's biscuits, felt or tweed hats, Europe-made shoes (patent leather, brown leather & tennis), patent harness and carriage rugs'.

Chow Kit & Co, Kuala Lumpur's first department store, stocked a good range of cigars—Londres, Regalia, Chica, Princesas, High Life in the East, Damas, Nuevo Habano, Senoritas, Windsors, 2a Habano Colon, Dalagos Medianos & Rangoon.

And teas—Assam, Ceylon, Johor and China.

It also sold tobacco and cigarettes of various kinds; electroplated wares; strong fireproof iron safes; commodes; office chairs and footstools; and horse food—gram, oats, padi, etc.

Even then, items made of rattan, found in abundance in today's interior decor shops, were popular. The shop sold rattan and bamboo basketwork of various kinds, office paper baskets, tiffin baskets, waste paper baskets, clothes baskets, bottle baskets and hand baskets.

The advertisement in the *Selangor Journal* ended thus: 'Orders and complaints promptly attended to!' The managing partner's name was given: Low Cheng Koon.

In *The Malay Mail* on 14 December 1896, the department store ran an advertisement: 'Chow Kit & Co invite the attention of the public to their new stock of goods comprising an excellent selection of X'mas toys, pipes, drapery, etc.'

The items sold at the department store reflected the Westernised tastes of the owner, Loke Chow Kit, an English-educated self-made millionaire who sent two sons to study in a boarding school in Scotland.

A self-made millionaire ...

Just a few doors away, Boon Ean & Co, at No. 10 Market Street, sold more or less similar items, but it had wines and spirits too.

To quench their thirst, colonial shoppers could buy Buchanan's and Usher's whiskey, claret, Hock, Hennessey's and Exshaw's brandy, sherry (White Seal), Bass's Light Oriental, Ale (Green Diamond), Tivoli beer, Bull Dog and Burke's stout, Cockburn and Campbell's port, Green and Yellow Chartreuse, Benedictine (D.O.M.), Chablis, Cherry brandy and Curacao.

The teetotaller could opt for lime juice cordial or Perak and Penang Aerated Waters, a soda drink.

Boon Ean & Co was also the sole agent for Mrs A. Jansen's pickles, mangoes and limes of the best quality. The shop's manager was Tan Cheng Whatt.

Java Jive

While the Chinese settled east of the confluence of the Gombak and Klang rivers along Klyne Street, High Street, Ampang Street, Old Market Square, Sultan Street, Petaling Street and Cecil Street, the Malays settled north of the confluence.

That explained the naming of Java Street and nearby Malay Street. A Boyanese *kongsi* was situated along Java Street and north of the street was a village called Kampung Rawa.

That short street near the Malay cemetery evolved into one of the town's busiest shopping roads, probably as busy as Petaling Street, in the early part of the 20th century. While the latter catered to the Chinese, Java Street became a shopping haven for the Europeans who in the early years of Kuala Lumpur also did their shopping at Market Street.

The Malay Mail reported on 25 November 1903 that 'Java Street is not much to look at, in fact it has been called the slum of slums of our local paradise, yet it is a street of no little activity; for in it are congregated a large number of native shops which, to judge from the crowds continually around them, should be doing a roaring trade.'

Later on, it was renamed Mountbatten Road (now called Jalan Tun Perak) and posh department stores like Robinson's, Whiteaways Laidlaw, John Little and Gian Singh were located there. Whiteaways was at the junction of Java Street and Malay Street in a multistorey building that was constructed in 1926 by Sehested and Neilsen, a Danish engineering and contracting firm.

Christmases were rather grand as the entire road was festooned with colourful lights and baubles, somewhat like Oxford Street in London. Thousands of people would be milling around the shopping street.

Over the years, its popularity as a shopping area declined. Robinson's closed and the stately building was demolished to make way for a skyscraper occupied by the Bank of Commerce (now called Bumiputra Commerce Bank). Slowly, the other stores shut down one by one.

As the sun set on Java Street, it rose on neighbouring Jalan Tuanku Abdul Rahman, which became Kuala Lumpur's Golden Mile.

The Whiteaways Laidlaw building was bought over by the Overseas Chinese Banking Corporation, which occupied it for a while. It has been left vacant for the past few years. On its facade, the words 'Bombay, Colombo, Madras, Rangoon, Calcutta, Singapore, Hong Kong, Penang and Nairobi' could be seen.

Recently, the bank embarked on a project to build a 20-storey office block at the site of the building and several adjoining shophouses.

The facades of the Whiteaways Laidlaw building and the adjoining shophouses were supposed to be saved, but they collapsed in September 1996. The facades were then demolished completely and now the bank plans to build replicas of the facades for the sake of the architectural heritage of the city.

With the opening of the nearby Masjid Jamek LRT station, there is hope that the glorious days of Java Street will be revived.

The 20-Million-Dollar Man

Loke Mansion
Medan Tuanku

Loke Yew is remembered as a party
animal and philanthropist.

The rags-to-riches stories of the first-generation overseas Chinese have always fired the imaginations of Malaysians, especially those who equate accumulation of wealth with success and achievement. Indeed, many entrepreneurs have been inspired by such legends.

Loke Yew was the archetypal Chinaman millionaire who was born into a peasant family and rose to become the richest man in the era after Yap Ah Loy. His legacy is in the form of his life-story and his fabulous mansion which still stands today at Medan Tuanku. It was renamed The Artiquarium in 1991 and housed an antique shop and an advertising agency. In 1999, it was given yet another moniker, International House Kuala Lumpur.

Loke Yew was born on 9 October 1846 to a peasant family in China and like many other Chinese, he set sail for Singapore in 1858. He was then 11 years old.

After working for four years as a shop assistant, he managed to save $99, which he reinvested into his own shop, Chop Heng Loong. Somehow, he made his way to Larut in Perak where he got involved in the civil war and managed to smuggle supplies past the blockade by hiring Orang Asli (aborigines) who knew secret jungle trails. This way, he sent in supplies and made lots of money and when his war chest had reached $140,000, he pumped it into opening tin mines in Perak.

Fickle fate ...

However, fate can be fickle, and his fortunes dipped when the price of tin collapsed. A man of resource and determination, he struggled on and started using steam-powered pumps to dig deeper into his Kinta Valley mines.

He recovered his losses, made even more money and moved south to Selangor where he became the chief tax farmer and tin miner.

For the next 20 years, he was Kuala Lumpur's richest and most powerful man.

Loke Yew owned tin mines, rubber plantations and properties. He had interests in Kuala Lumpur, Bentong, Selangor and Singapore. In Bentong, he even issued his own bank notes.

He became a member of the Selangor State Council and sat on numerous committees and chambers of commerce. He was also a great philanthropist.

Among his business associates were Choo Kia Peng, who started off as his clerk, and Robson, who was the founder of *The Malay Mail*, today's only afternoon tabloid in the Klang Valley.

Wild Parties

A workaholic, Loke Yew could never really divorce himself from his businesses. On 24 February 1917, while he was in one of his rubber estates, he caught the malarial bug which killed him. By then, his business empire was worth $20 million.

Loke Yew's mansion at Batu Road was eclectic. He had bought it in 1892 but some parts of it date back to 1860 when it was then owned by Cheow Ah Yeok, Yap Ah Loy's crony. When the King of Siam and the Sultan of Kedah visited Kuala Lumpur in May 1890, the Siamese royal guest stayed at Towkay Ah Yeok's mansion while the Kedah sultan put up at Yap Ah Loy's house. Towkay Ah Yeok died in December 1892 and that was when Loke Yew bought the mansion and 10 acres of land planted with rubber and coconut trees from his estate.

Loke Yew was somewhat of an enigma. There were reports that he loved the quiet life and hated ostentation; yet some said that he was a great swinger and entertainer who threw some of the wildest parties in town. A list of Who's Who turned up at his mansion to be feted in style and splendour.

The Malay Mail's gossip page reported on 2 April 1897: 'A first-class repast was served at Towkay Loke Yew's house and by the time that the champagne, hock, liqueurs and whiskey had all amicably mixed, the company exhausted all their vocal and oratorical powers and accordingly adjourned to the Malay theatre.'

Aid in Hong Kong

Loke Yew's legacy reaches beyond the borders of Malaysia—he is remembered even in Hong Kong.

In the Hong Kong University, there is a bronze bust of the Malayan tycoon and the Great Hall has been renamed Loke Yew Hall.

This memorial was the university's way of thanking the tycoon for his financial aid to the institution.

In 1916, Loke donated $50,000 and extended an interest-free 20-year loan of $500,000 to the university. Like many other rich Chinese businessmen of his era, Loke Yew was not well educated and though he was cosmopolitan in outlook, he could barely speak English. Having made it rich, his way to repay society was by donating to institutions of higher learning.

He was awarded an honorary degree of Doctor of Laws by the University of Hong Kong on 4 January 1917, but about a month later, Loke Yew died.

It was the university's highest honour for a 'Chinese gentleman in the Federated Malay States'.

The university commissioned English sculptor Charles d'Orville Pilkington Jacson to make the bust in 1955.

Loke Yew's philanthropy is well known. When World War I broke out, he offered free rice to passers-by.

He also received recognition from the British. He became a Companion of the Most Distinguished Order of St. Michael and St. George.

It was also reported, however, that 'as a man, he particularly disliked ostentatiousness in any form, lived very quietly and was always at work. He had no leisure and no particular hobbies'. He was also reported to have kept old cars, gone to his office in rickshas and was the 'least expensively-dressed man'. Then again, he was often seen wearing a black Panama hat and shiny black Chinese suit.

Loke Yew was never really satisfied with his mansion and spent a dozen years constantly renovating it. Since he had travelled three times to Europe, he borrowed ideas from some of the grand homes that he had seen which explains the European influence in the mansion.

It was only in April 1904 that he was sufficiently satisfied with his home and, to mark the occasion, popped the cork and threw a party. *The Malay Mail* reported that it was 'quite a housewarming'.

Another report described the house thus: 'Towkay Loke Yew's new house on the Batu Road is one of the most palatial residences in town. Nothing but chengal timber has been used for floors, doors, posts, etc, while the upper and lower verandahs are paved with specially imported Chinese tiles.'

Peace and Prosperity

The main hall had a very high ceiling while the dining room had space for 20 tables or at least 200 guests. Socialite Loke Yew had his priorities right.

While the house had a European exterior, its interior displayed Chinese influences. Loke Yew commissioned artist Wang Lien Fung to paint the scenes in the house. Inside there was a moon gate on top of which were the Chinese characters: 'Gallop Through the Perfumed Fields'.

At the front door, there was a plaque in Chinese which read: 'Garden of Peace and Prosperity'.

Loke Yew's last wife lived in the mansion with their children till she migrated to Switzerland in 1930. Loke Yew's son, Loke Wan Tho, who was born in the mansion in 1915 died in a plane crash in Taiwan in 1964.

The mansion remained empty for 11 years till the Japanese Occupation, when the invaders used it as their headquarters. After the war, it was used by the San Min Chu Yi Youth Corps as a Chinese school and, in 1948, the police turned it into a Special Branch training school till 1958.

The 10 acres of land surrounding the mansion were auctioned off for $10 million in 1963 to Malayan Finance Corp. Ltd. One of the directors of the company was Choo Kok Leong, who had married one of Loke Yew's granddaughters.

The mansion was abandoned until 1971 when the Samat Art Gallery and Asia Antiques shop started operating on the ground floor. On the first floor was the Malaysia College of Music. These establishments remained until the late 70s. In February 1991, advertising mogul Datuk Lim Kok Wing turned the vacant house into The Artiquarium. It became known as the International House Kuala Lumpur in 1991 and was a world-class institution for English Language lessons. Exhibitions showcasing the illustrations of students from colleges run by Datuk Lim were also held there.

The Spotted Dog Evolves into an Asian Thoroughbred

The Selangor Club
Jalan Raja

Selangor Club has seen a coterie of
planters and lawyers.

Selangor Club—a splash of elegance in the heart of the city.

In the late 19th century, the Selangor Club was where the action was—everybody who was anybody was a member. It was where white planters and colonial administrators quenched their thirst with several rounds of *stengahs* and where bored womenfolk held their gossip sessions.

It was the meeting place for romantic trysts, and where one could find out the latest news. There was a report of 'ladies sitting in a ring on the verandah (who) were wont to discuss the well-worn subjects of the price of ducks and the delinquencies of the "boy".'

There were potluck parties where participating ladies and their 'boys' would turn up with cakes, salads, pies, cold cuts, sandwiches and other victuals.

St. Andrew's Night and Christmas were gala events when merrymaking lasted till the wee hours, gallons of spirits were imbibed and everybody had rollicking fun. A typical menu during such gala dinners comprised 'stuffed eggs, tinned mulligatawny soup, red snapper and scraggy chicken'. And, of course, beer, wine, gin, whiskey, brandy and whatever the bar had in stock.

A visitor to the Selangor Club today can be excused for assuming that it is a club for affluent Indian and Punjabi lawyers given the strikingly large number of them fraternising there. The Spotted Dog has evolved over the years, becoming more Asian in character. And the planters' club has become more like a lawyers' club.

Founded in 1884 to meet the needs of the Europeans, the Selangor Club was formed as a social and cricket club featuring the all-important bar, with reading rooms and billiard halls. Its original wooden clubhouse and stables were at the northern end of the Parade Ground where St. Mary's Church now stands.

Robson, who stepped foot in Kuala Lumpur in 1889, later recalled that the Selangor Club was 'a small wooden building with atap roof where heads of department played billiards with their chief clerks'.

Acting Resident Rodger, who had energetically pushed for the formation of the club, became its first President while Venning was the first secretary.

At that time, Rodger was merely acting as Resident and his actual post was Commissioner of Lands. Provision was made in the constitution of the Selangor Club that the Commissioner of Lands should be Vice-president *ex officio* so that Rodger could remain when Swettenham resumed his post as Resident.

A year after the club's foundation, the government lent it $900 to enlarge its building.

The new clubhouse was then built at the present-day site in 1889. It was a two-storied structure and the upper floor was used for dances and concerts.

In 1889, Count Bernstorff became the first salaried secretary of the club but his performance left much to be desired. In fact, he left with some money too. Some $1,100 of the club's funds went missing during his stint and soon after he left, there were stories *Missing money ...* circulating that he became aide-de-camp to the Chinese Viceroy in north China. In that dark hour of Selangor Club's history, some senior officials left and founded the Lake Club.

The Other Club

The history of the Lake Club is interlinked with that of Selangor Club. All 28 founding members of the Lake Club had been with the Selangor Club and they formed their own extremely exclusive and colour-conscious institution in 1890 for at least two reasons.

According to Gullick, it was another sign of the tendency towards class and communal differentiation that led to the formation of the Lake Club, which had its clubhouse in the Lake Gardens beside Club Road, today's Jalan Parlimen.

The second reason could have been that they were fed up with the way the Selangor Club was run, especially in the handling of its finances.

Thus the white-only Lake Club took form and that attitude of white supremacy lasted for a good many years and it was only in 1958 that non-whites were admitted as members. The first Malaysian President took office only in 1965.

In the old days, the Lake Club's membership list comprised the cream of colonial society. Prominent personalities who were members included State Treasurer Venning; founder of the Selangor Fire Brigade H.F. Bellamy; police chief H.C. Syers; the first Selangor State Engineer and later General Manager of the Federated Malay States Railway C.E. Spooner; founder of *The Malay Mail* J.H.M. Robson; District Officer of Kuala

Lumpur and later British Adviser to Johor D.G. Campbell; Dr E.A.O. Travers; W.E. Maxwell, first Resident-General of the Federated Malay States and later Governor of the Straits Settlements; and High Commissioner of the Federated Malay States F.A. Swettenham.

Not only was it snobbish, but it had strict dress codes too—members had to wear long-sleeved shirts with neckties during the day and full suits at night. It was only much later that the club allowed batik shirts.

In 1985, the by then Malaysianised club, was expanded and renamed Royal Lake Club. Despite the 'royal' tag, it had lost much of its snobbishness.

Henry Huttenbach took over as secretary and nursed the club back to health. By 1892, its finances were much improved and the number of members increased to 140.

This coincided with a boom in coffee planting and the number of planters among its members went up dramatically. In fact, Huttenbach himself was a coffee planter.

The Selangor Club was almost exclusively European in membership though certain outstanding natives were members too.

Plum-Pudding Dogs

Its sobriquet was the Spotted Dog and there are a few theories on its origin. One has it that police chief Syer's wife had two dalmatians which were often spotted sprinting behind her carriage while she went to and from the club, and these 'plum-pudding dogs' were the source of the club's nickname. Another has it that the first emblem of the club was a clumsy rendition of a spotted leopard which many thought was a spotted dog.

The third possible reason is racist. This relates to the fact that early members of the Selangor Club included non-whites such as Sultan Abdul Samad, Yap Ah Loy and Thamboosamy

Pillai plus some working class Europeans 'of rough exterior' who were railway workers.

Someone had remarked that 'frequenters of the Spotted Dog must accept the company as they find it'.

Some members felt so uncomfortable with these 'spots' in the club that they decided to leave and form their own exclusively white — and more genteel — club in 1890.

The 'spots' in the club ...

Since the Selangor Club was within walking distance of the government offices, it was only natural that it was a watering hole for civil servants. Since most lawyers then were Europeans, they turned up at the club too.

Dispensing Good Spirits

Other than the Selangor Club, many Europeans also frequented Maynards, a pharmaceutical shop.

It was probably not the high quality medicines that attracted the crowd. More likely, they turned up for the wines, spirits and liqueurs.

Robson said that in 1889 and the early part of the 1890s, the only European shop in Kuala Lumpur was Maynards near the Market Street Bridge, which sold medicines, provisions and drinks. 'The place was a rendezvous for Europeans.'

Maynards was sold to D. Macreath, a chemist, on 16 April 1894 and he renamed it The Dispensary. He stocked very much the same list of things such as 'brewed ginger beer, Tennant's pale ale, Tennant's stout, G.A. & Co's light shandy (beer and lemonade), dark shandy (stout and tonic) and Devonshire cider'.

The Dispensary also sold Manila cigars of the best brands 'always in good condition'; revolvers; cartridge cases and ammunition; spectacles and eye glasses 'to suit all sights'; photographic chemicals; filters; infants' and invalids' foods; toilet requisites and 'every modern convenience and luxury for the nursery and sick room'. Since it was The Dispensary, it also prescribed and sold medicines.

The white planters who were in remote areas and were left out of the social circuit would make it a point to go to the Selangor Club to catch up on things when they were in town.

Most planters would be in Kuala Lumpur once a month for appointments with their bankers to withdraw money for their workers' salaries. There was an informal agreement amongst them to turn up in Kuala Lumpur—and the club—on the first Saturday of every month for drinks.

Rubber planter Henri Fauconnier recalled that after completing his business at the bank, he would have a haircut at the club's barber.

He continued: 'I made my way to the bar. It was packed. The semicircular counter, edged by an unbroken line of lifted elbows was inaccessible. But beyond it were a few little cane tables and chairs for those whose thirst was not so urgent. The company always arranged itself in geographical order and I was familiar with the zone of occupation assigned to my district.'

He described a particularly rollicking night: 'Three cheers were given, followed by the cry of the Malayan tiger, Rrrrrraumph, then all in a circle, with joined hands and marking time with their elbows, they sang *For He's a Jolly Good Fellow...*'

Fire destroyed the main part of the clubhouse in December 1970 and it was rebuilt eight years later. The new two-storied building in mock-Tudor style, in keeping with the earlier structure's design, had a basement carpark and was built at a cost of RM3 million.

When it celebrated its centenary, there was a huge sign erected which read: '100 Not Out.' Few people, other than cricketers, understood that term.

Now more than a century old, the club has shown no signs of ageing and is still as handsome as ever.

Rehashing the Hash Story

Panting runners follow a trail of paper planted by a 'hare' who sometimes leads the runners astray. But that is part of the fun. The runners usually end where they begin and then the party starts—meals (Western or local) are served buffet-style and the six-packs, chilled to perfection, are opened. Often, these parties last till the wee hours of the morning after the participants have exhausted their supply of jokes and beer.

These regular work-out and *yam seng* (a Chinese toast somewhat akin to 'bottoms up') sessions are organised by the Hash House Harriers (Harrietes for the ladies)—who comprise a bunch of fun-lovers who like to combine their health consciousness with their penchant for having a good time.

Selangor Club has the honour of being the Mother Hash for that was where the first chapter of the Hash House Harrier (HHH) story began in 1938.

The origin of hashing is shrouded in a colourful cocktail of fact and fiction. Legend has it that a group of Englishmen and Australians were at the Spotted Dog on a Monday night nursing a hangover from the weekend's revelries when they suddenly had a brilliant idea—perhaps they would feel better if they had a run to work off the alcohol from their bodies. So they had their run—and felt better. Not only did their actions adversely affect the sales of hangover medication, but A.S. Gispert, Cecil Lee, 'Horse' Thomson, 'Torch' Bennett and Philip Wickens started an institution.

The concept of runners following a paper trail was not a new one then. The British had been running informally in groups through jungle and rubber estates since the 1920s. There had been running clubs before in Kuala Lumpur, which faded from the scene in 1934, and Johor Baru, which lasted from 1932 to 1935.

There were also hare and hound clubs such as the Kinta Harriers in Ipoh and the Springgit Harriers in Malacca circa 1935, but these were short-lived. In

Shanghai and Kuching clubs, participants followed paper trails on horseback.

In 1932, Thomson ran in a club with no name which followed rules that were essentially like Hash rules. This club closed in 1935. In Malacca, Gispert was in the Springgit Harriers which was formed in 1935 and among those who ran with him was Bennett.

In 1938, Gispert, Thomson and Lee were in Kuala Lumpur and met up at the Spotted Dog and decided to form the running club which they named Hash House Harriers. The maiden run was held in the last week of December 1938.

The Spotted Dog had another sobriquet at that time—Hash House. It was called that because of the unpalatable (some Selangor Club members considered themselves gourmets) food it served.

Technically, Bennett was not a founder-member because he was on leave when the HHH was formally formed while Wickens joined in 1939.

Gispert, who was one of the prime movers behind the HHH, died in February 1942 at the age of 38 during the Japanese invasion of Singapore.

After the war, the HHH picked up the pieces and the weekly fun-runs started again and became increasingly popular.

Expatriates who worked and hashed in Kuala Lumpur started chapters of the HHH when they returned to their home countries. Now there are 1,700 HHH chapters in 160 countries. In Malaysia alone, there are 110 Hash chapters.

In October 1998, the 60th anniversary of the Hash House Harriers was celebrated in Kuala Lumpur and 5,700 hashers from 60 countries turned up at the Mother Hash to participate in the running and partake of the good spirits.

While the doors of the HHH have always been open to the ladies, at least one Harrier in Penang felt uncomfortable and encountered 'some embarrassing moments because of women running and suffered distress and severe mental anguish'.

On 29 June 1990, florist Toh Boon Leng obtained an injunction to restrain the Penang Hash House Harriers from letting women run with them.

However, a few days later, the High Court dismissed the injunction in a landmark decision for women's liberationists. Justice Datuk Edgar Joseph Jr said the matter was trifle and was a storm in a tea cup.

'If the plaintiff is troubled by the women's presence in the Monday runs, all he has to do is stay away from those runs,' he ruled.

Harriers and Harrietes have been lawfully hashing together ever since.

Commoner's Club

Lake Club catered to the *creme de la creme* of white society in 1890s Kuala Lumpur, while the Selangor Club was for the middle-classes.

It was this kind of discrimination that led those who were denied admission to both clubs to form the Selangor Recreation Club in 1896.

The early members included some rough and rowdy whites like the British mechanics, engine-drivers, prison warders and a few Malayan 'natives' from the civil service. Considered low-brow and uncultured, they had fun anyway sipping *stengahs* at their own bar and playing billiards and darts.

The first president of the club was Dr Travers. British Resident Rodger and Towkay Loke Yew both contributed $100 to the building fund. Rodger officially opened the clubhouse, a humble wooden shed, on 13 February 1897.

Today, it has about 105 members, many of whom are retired civil servants. The clubhouse was demolished in late 1999 to make way for Phase Two of the Merdeka Square project, which involves the construction of Kuala Lumpur's first electronic library and gallery.

Club members now meet in Bukit Kiara.

The Grand Old Lady

Bangunan Sultan Abdul Samad
Jalan Raja

The beloved symbol of Kuala Lumpur is
ageless and evergreen.

Bangunan Sultan Abdul Samad's magnificent facade.

Kuala Lumpur's Grand Old Lady is very pretty, especially at night. Even though she is around a hundred years old, she needs no makeup. Her blemishes and wrinkles are not visible and dozens of photographers snap shots of her daily from various angles and leave with good memories of having been in her presence.

The Bangunan (Building) Sultan Abdul Samad can be seen on postcards, tourism brochures, posters, stamps, paintings and even on small ceramic plates sold at souvenir shops. It is the beloved symbol of Kuala Lumpur.

The grand building faces the Spotted Dog with the Dataran Merdeka (the Padang) separating them. That rectangle of grass encapsulates the history of Kuala Lumpur as much as the confluence of the Gombak and Klang rivers just behind Bangunan Sultan Abdul Samad and the early settlements around Market Square. It is the historical heart of the city, especially from the colonial administrators' point of view.

One British architect recently commented on 'the total fantasy of the nearly theatrical setting, the only theatrical setting ever devised for British administration in the wide range of the Empire'.

At night, the Bangunan Abdul Samad, which now houses the Supreme Court, is lit up by hundreds of bulbs turning the area into a fairyland of lights. On Saturdays, the section of Jalan Raja (called Gombak Road in the past) in front of the building is fenced off and turned into a pedestrian mall. Often, people buy food and drinks at the *pasar malam* which is held every Saturday at nearby Jalan Tuanku Abdul Rahman and have a feast on the road.

It is hard to imagine what Kuala Lumpur would be like without Bangunan Sultan Abdul Samad. It is even harder to imagine that some town planner had actually thought the unthinkable and had suggested demolishing it to build a modern concrete-and-glass shoebox in its place. Thankfully, somebody in power had the wisdom and foresight to throw that plan out of the window where it belonged.

The builders and architects of the Grand Old Lady would have turned in their graves.

Instead, the building and surrounding structures were refurbished and spruced up. The black domes of the building, which were apparently painted black during World War II to make them less visible to enemy planes, were replaced with copper plates.

In the Vicinity

The Moorish-styled buildings around Bangunan Sultan Abdul Samad are among the oldest in Kuala Lumpur and each opens a different page in the city's history.

Most were government buildings completed in 1896 to complement the main government office (later called Bangunan Sultan Abdul Samad).

Behind the former GPO is the Industrial Court which was formerly the first department store in Kuala Lumpur—Chow Kit & Co. Built in the early 1890s, its site was chosen because it was only a short walk from the Klang river and was a convenient place to unload supplies sent by boat upriver from Klang.

The Government took over the building before World War II and in the mid-1950s, it was the Federal Establishment Office. Later it housed the Ministry of Transport and after that, the Registry of Societies.

It was then tastefully renovated and turned into the Industrial Court and the impressive timber staircase inside was restored. Five court rooms, separate chambers for the president and a library were also built.

Across Lebuh Pasar Besar (the old Market Street), is the Infokraf building, designed by A.C. Norman, which has a permanent display of Malaysian handicraft items for tourists and a souvenir shop. Its original occupant, when it was built in 1896, was the headquarters of the Federated Malay States Railway. It was later expanded to house the Selangor Public Works Department. Much later, the Bank Pertanian (Agriculture Bank) and the PWD had their offices there.

Across the Gombak river is the High Court building, built in 1904 and designed by A.C. Norman. A fire destroyed the High Court building in December 1992. However, case hearings continued at Bangunan Sultan Abdul Samad and the process of law was not derailed.

It has since been renovated into a five-storied structure to house eight High Courts, an Appeal Court, six judges' chambers and several Sessions Courts.

Next to it is the former City Hall building, another A.C. Norman design dating back to 1896. Originally housing the KL Sanitary Board, it became the KL Municipality in 1948. It then evolved into the City Hall and the city administrators shifted in soon after. It also housed a theatre for many years.

Adjoining it is a long narrow building with an impressive facade of arches facing Jalan Tun Perak (formerly Java Street). This was the Information Department and was built by Norman in 1909. It was used by the Federated Malay States Survey Department and later the Tourist Development Corporation before the Information Department moved in.

The old City Hall and Information Department buildings have undergone an RM20-million conversion into a lower courts complex housing 30 Magistrate's and Sessions Courts.

A bridge was built recently to link Bangunan Sultan Abdul Samad with the former General Post Office (which is now located at Dayabumi, a short walk away) and thankfully the architect was sensitive to the Moorish designs of the two buildings.

The existing building was constructed between October 1894 and April 1897 under Norman's supervision.

Today, the Bangunan Sultan Abdul Samad looks elegant and grand, befitting its status as a symbol of the city.

Oriental Style

Though A.C. Norman has been credited with the design of the building, he was not directly responsible for the Moorish architecture.

He had drawn ground plans for the building and a Mr Bidwell drew an elevation in classical Renaissance, but their boss, Mr C.E. Spooner, State Engineer and Director of the Public Works Department, changed the plans.

'Though I did not like the design, I adopted the arrangement of the offices and the general lines. I then decided on the Mohametan (sic) style and in due course sent it in with an estimate for $152,000,' Mr Spooner was later reported as saying.

A Mohammedan style ...

Mr Spooner, who had earlier served in Ceylon, felt that an oriental style was more in keeping with the tropical environment.

The foundation stone was laid by the Governor of the Straits Settlements, Sir Charles B.H. Mitchell, on 6 October 1894.

The *Selangor Journal* reported: 'Decorations were the order of the day, and an arch at the entrance to the ground, festoons of flags and plan-adorned walls gave as gay an aspect as possible to what is never a very cheerful sight—the beginning of a large building.'

The Governor said: 'It is a grand thing to build fine public offices worthy of the Service, but the services should then be worthy of the home given them.'

A.C. Norman then presented the Governor with 'a very handsome silver trowel, with ivory handle and gold bands'.

In a cavity below the foundation stone, the Governor placed a yen, some Straits coins, a piece of Selangor tin from the Straits Trading Company and a copy of the current edition of the *Selangor Journal*.

Above the foundation stone was built 'a handsome clock tower 140 feet (43 metres) high, in the Arabesque style, which is to form the main feature of the front'. Two other towers, containing circular staircases, forming 'handsome additions to either facade' were built with the clock tower in the middle.

The two-storied building had 3.7-metre-wide verandahs and was constructed of red bricks with imitation stone dressings and a tiled roof. The government offices were officially opened in April 1897.

On the ground floor were the Public Works Department and District Offices, Mines Department, Lands, Audit, and

Treasury, with each office having its own vault. The Post Office and the Sanitary Board were located there too. On the first floor, there were offices of the Secretariat, a State Council Room, a Sanitary Board Hall, rooms for the Resident and other officials and the Chinese Secretariat.

Over the years, all sorts of government departments have been located there. The list includes the Federal Treasury, the Attorney-General's Office and the Accountant-General's Office. Anxious couples used to queue up there to legalise their relationships at the Marriage Registry. It now houses the Supreme Court.

Some 4 million bricks, 2,500 barrels of cement, 18,000 pikuls of lime, 5,000 pounds of copper, 50 tons of steel and iron and 30,000 cubic feet of timber were used to construct the building. At $152,000, it was a bargain even at 1897 prices. Now, it is priceless.

Reader's Corner

The Kuala Lumpur Memorial Library is situated in a heritage building that used to house the government's printer's office.

Built in 1909, the building is a contrast from the Moorish buildings that surround it. Awnings which were built about 50 years ago give the building a daintily odd character.

Architects have labelled its design as neo-Renaissance, and some think that the building is based on Mr Bidwell's original design for the Sultan Abdul Samad building. City Hall spent RM4 million renovating the building and many original structures like the metal pillars inside were left intact.

The library officially opened on 29 March 1989, and started off with a collection of 19,000 books. It also offered research and exhibition facilities on Kuala Lumpur. Since its opening, it has become a chess centre too, and has hosted numerous tournaments.

Field of Independence

Dataran Merdeka
Jalan Raja

The Padang has always been the heart
and soul of the city.

The Cop's fountain, Merdeka Square

One of the first places where tourists will be dropped off
in a city tour of Kuala Lumpur is Dataran Merdeka
(Merdeka Square). They will be shown the floral park at one
end where the Roman columns and fountains are. At the other
end, they will see a huge flagpole which, as the tour guide will
undoubtedly inform them, is the tallest in the world.

The Cop's Fountain

The fountain at the corner of the Padang opposite the Standard Chartered Bank was built in 1897, in memory of Steve Harper, an inspector of the Selangor Military Police. It was put up by the Sanitary Board at a cost of $500–$600.

It functioned till 1950. Over the years, several attempts to get it to work again failed. It was left unused and in the 1970s and 1980s, it became a huge flower pot. The pool was filled with earth and flowering plants were planted in it.

When the Dataran Merdeka project was completed in late 1989, it was dismantled and reassembled several metres away. The fountain has been functioning ever since.

The field itself, replanted with ornamental grass, is out of bounds most of the time and these days only gardeners, crows and other birds step on it.

The spick and span new-look Merdeka Square is like a typical showpiece—formal, structured and impressive. But in its previous guise as Selangor Padang, it had more soul and was certainly more colourful.

Even in 1905, it was reported in *The Malay Mail* that the one showplace of noble buildings was the Padang. 'When a steeple has been added to the church, the Padang will be flanked on three sides by buildings not unworthy of the capital of the Federated Malay States.'

In 1880, the Padang was not 'the level and even sward' which Dataran Merdeka now is. The northern part, near where the Anglican Church stands today, and the section opposite it was swampy, and much of the flat land was a clearing used for vegetable cultivation and fruit trees. H.C. Syers, the superintendent of police, used to shoot snipe at the northern end in the mornings.

Police were stationed in Kuala Lumpur under the able leadership of Syers in 1875. Syers was a remarkable man—when he took over as Inspector of Police in Selangor, he was only 23 years old.

Inspector at 23 ...

When the police headquarters, called the Fort, was built at Bluff Road, the barracks for policemen were constructed nearby on lower ground, somewhere near where Jalan Tangsi is today.

The police used the flat centre portion of the nearby field for drills and parades and that was why it became known as the Parade Ground. It was only after the original Selangor Club was built in 1884, where St. Mary's Church now stands, that it became known as Club Padang or simply the Padang and later, Selangor Padang.

During the building boom of the 1880s, a brickkiln was built on or near the Padang and Yap Ah Loy had his prison somewhere near the site of Standard Chartered Bank (then called Chartered Bank of India, Australia and China).

Big, Strong and Friendly

To many Malaysians, banking is Standard Chartered. This is because the established bank has been operating in the peninsula since the early days of Kuala Lumpur's development.

As early as 1888, the bank—then called the Chartered Bank of India, Australia and China—had a branch in Kuala Lumpur.

Its reputation as a safe and solid bank was further cemented by a memorable series of advertisements in the print and television media in the 1970s which featured a giant Sikh guard and the slogan 'Big, Strong, Friendly.' The slogan has lived on in the minds of Malaysians although that particular advertising campaign was discontinued a long time ago.

To solve the problem of having a reliable banking system, the Chartered Bank of India, Australia and

China was invited to operate in Kuala Lumpur by the Government and in 1888, it set up a branch at a shophouse at Clark Street (now called Jalan Mahkamah Tinggi). Its building near the Padang was completed in 1891, and that site was chosen because it was near the police headquarters at Bluff Road (now Jalan Bukit Aman) and hence, could be easily guarded.

Little was done to level the Padang till the Chinese houses facing it were demolished in 1894 to make way for the construction of the Government Offices.

It was when Ernest Birch took over as Resident in 1892 that the Padang was levelled and made suitable for cricket games and other sports. Ernest Birch was a keen cricketer and was chiefly responsible for making the game popular in Kuala Lumpur.

Trying to Fit an Oval Into a Rectangle

Cricket, that quintessential British sport, was so important to the colonial administrators that they often selected recruits based on their ability to play the game.

Cricket in KL received a boost with the arrival of (later Sir) Ernest Birch who came to act as Resident after the departure of Maxwell in 1892. Ernest Birch, son of J.W.W. Birch, who was murdered as Resident of Perak in 1875, had come to the Straits Settlements around 1880.

In Singapore, he excelled in cricket and his dexterity in the game was noted in official records. Thus, during his stint in KL, he got his priorities right and 'the raising and turfing of a portion of the Parade Ground was completed, the cricket pitch was formed and put in good order, and the swamp at the lower end of the ground near the Chartered Bank was partially filled'.

Cricket was played as early as 1884, but the preparation of a proper 'square' for pitches and improvements date from the time Birch took over as Resident.

Generally cricket was played with seriousness but in 1893, a light-hearted match reportedly occurred between ladies and men. To make it equal, the men were to bowl and field with their left hands only and to bat with broomsticks.

The Resident's wife started the Ladies' innings and was soon out for a duck. Other members of the ladies' team fared almost as badly and the men, to be expected, won the rather boisterous game.

The reporter offered his helpful opinion: 'One concluding word of advice to the ladies; the grand rule of whist, silence, should also be observed while fielding.'

Cricket was an obsession, and many a job seeker would be asked if he played the game. If he did, he stood a better chance of being employed than the other applicant who did not.

This colonial tradition filtered down to the natives and very soon playing cricket at the Padang was the dream of almost every schoolboy.

The Padang has been graced by some of cricket's great names such as David Gower, Rohan Kanhar, Lesley Hall, Farouk Engineer and Sir Gary Sobers.

Fans still recall the game in 1964 when Sir Gary was bowled first ball, in other words a 'first ball duck,' by legspinner Dr Alex Delilkan.

Old-timers will recall the 1927 game when an All-Malayan 11 beat a strong Australian team.

Playing cricket at the Padang was so prestigious that parents would buy their sons new flannels when they made their debut at the holy ground of Malaysian cricket. Cricketers would dress up for the occasion by wearing sparkling clean garments. It was a major event in a cricketer's life, a coming of age of sorts.

In 1988, there was a hue and cry when cricketers, many of whom were Selangor Club members, found out that their holy ground would be dug up to make way for an underground parking project. They were afraid that when the new padang was created, it would be too small for cricket to be played on. During this uproar, they discovered that the Padang had never been large enough for a proper cricket oval anyway.

For the hundred years before that, cricketers at the Padang had been trying to fit an oval into a rectangle which was never wide enough to begin with.

The Padang measured 259 metres by 113 metres. The Dataran Merdeka measured 172 metres by 97.5 metres, because there was a tiled walkway around the field and a section at the southern end was allocated for the giant flagpole. A proper cricket oval measures 160 metres by 142 metres. The Padang was long enough, but it was never wide enough for cricket—the holy ground of the game had never been perfect.

But that did not deter the cricketers. A final game between Royal Selangor Club and Kunta Kinte Cricket Club in a Stoner Shield match was held on 8 May 1988 before the bulldozers scarred the field forever.

However, there was good news for the fans of the sport. In May 1991, some 17 months after the Dataran Merdeka's official opening, workers started laying a 27 by 10.8-metre artificial turf on the field. During construction of Dataran Merdeka, the contractor had created a special concrete foundation for the wicket. But the original cow-grass had been replaced by the ornamental and more fragile zygosia grass and cricketers had to wear soft-soled shoes in order not to damage the turf.

Some time later, cricket was played again at the former Padang, but purists complained that it was not the same any more.

Upkeep and improvement of the Padang was the responsibility of the Sanitary Board from 1890 onwards and the levelling of the entire Padang was completed by 1895.

The Padang became the centre for all types of sports. In addition to the cricket pitch in the centre, there were two tennis courts near the club and football fields at the north and south ends.

KL's Underground

When the bulldozers and workers started work in the Padang, they were like ants tunnelling their way into the heart of Kuala Lumpur.

Removing the red earth by truckloads, the Padang was turned into a gigantic hole. And as a reminder of Kuala Lumpur's beginnings, the diggers struck tin. It had always been rumoured that beneath the Padang was a wealth of tin. The Land and Mines Department had to send officers to check on the workers to ensure that they were merely removing the earth and not mining the area.

Initially the plan was for a three-level underground complex of parking bays and shops. Due to time and financial constraints, a single-level underground parking area incorporating some shops at the southern end was built at a cost of RM20 million.

Work began in May 1988 and proceeded smoothly, though there was a slight delay initially due to a legal tangle between the main contractor and a sub-contractor. The surface level featuring the new-look padang with ornamental grass and giant flagpole was completed in October 1989, in time for the Commonwealth Heads of Government Meeting. The giant flagpole measures 102 metres and is the tallest in the world. The previous holder of the title, standing at 87.7 metres, is in Vancouver, Canada.

Beneath the hastily built, but still passably pretty surface, work continued for almost another year.

Underground, there were 615 parking bays, 26 hawker stalls and 83 shoplots. The shopkeepers opened for business with great expectancy of a goldrush of tourists. The rush came in the form of flood waters and the drainage in the area had to be improved.

Some time later, the shops closed one by one due to lack of business. Some had consulted *feng shui* masters and the culprits were identified as ancient trees in front of the main entrances which prevented good luck from entering the underground shops. Since they were regarded almost as heritage trees, they could not be chopped down and the shops kept on closing one by one.

Then a project to revive the underground commercial area was launched and the Plaza Putra was created. This project comprised a food court, fast food outlets, restaurants, cinemas and an indoor golf centre. Business picked up somewhat and there has not been much further development after that.

Recently, a drama centre was opened there, providing KL residents with a hall for plays and comedy sketches.

More than a century down the road, the Padang is still the centre of activities.

Muddy Pool

The Padang was also a centre of entertainment, with a bandstand for musical performances.

Comprising mainly Filipinos, the Police Band held concerts there twice a week. Selangor Club members were entertained to popular tunes of the time while they sipped their *stengahs*.

Whenever it rained heavily, the Klang river burst its banks and the low-lying Padang was often flooded. In 1926, a heavy torrent of rain turned the Padang into a huge muddy pool.

A silver-haired lawyer by the name of Ferri wagered that he could swim from the Selangor Club to the government offices without touching the ground.

He swam across the Padang ...

Ferri, whose office was at Klyne Street, apparently won the bet, but it was not recorded if his silver hair was tinted brown by the mud.

Chartered Bank tried to seal its underground vault with cement, but water seeped in and when the flood was over, its staff took out millions of dollars in currency notes to be dried in the sun on the Padang. Guards stood by on duty and it must have been such a sight to see all that money spread out like that.

In 1913, the coronation of King George V was celebrated at the Padang and associations, guilds and schoolchildren gathered there for the occasion. Shouts of 'God save the King!' were heard.

From 1918, Armistice Day celebrations were held at the Padang on 11 November every year. Members of the Malayan Service Volunteer Reserve, Malayan Volunteer Infantry, ex-servicemen and the police paraded at the Padang. It is not clear when this Armistice Day parade stopped.

There was always something happening at the Padang—a rugby game, a football match, cricket or a marching band performance. Even if there was nothing on, the bored KL resident could just relax on the field and chat with a friend or simply watch the world go by.

Cruising on the Green Carpet

The Selangor Padang has always been the centre of activities in Kuala Lumpur. Some were quite unwelcome, especially those that took place in the mid-1980s.

While the *pondans* strutted their stuff at one end of the Padang outside the Anglican Church, a different crowd gathered at the opposite end, where the fountain was located.

The gay community of Kuala Lumpur emerged from closets and gathered to, well, get to know each other better. The slang word for such activity is 'cruising'.

They even had their own name for the Padang—the Green Carpet. Cruising at the Green Carpet was the finale of their Saturday night revelries.

When the cops cracked down on the *pondans*, the gays were also intimidated and slowly became less visible. Some returned to the closet while others found clubs to cruise in.

Silence of the Girls

Recently, a big hoo-ha was made over *boh sia* girls hanging out at the ceremonial field.

'Boh sia' is Hokkien for 'no sound'. Nobody knows why or how that term came to be used to describe the sex-starved teenaged girls who hung out at the Padang and nearby Jalan Mahkamah Persekutuan. These promiscuous girls were said to enjoy picking up guys or luring them for some steamy sex.

Most of the guys who hung out there were bikers (called Mat Biker in Malay slang) who raced on the streets of the city, or long-haired grunge-rock lovers (called Mat Rock).

This new phenomena was condemned by the Government as symptomatic of the decaying social fabric of the secular, modern world and as another example of the hedonism of the West creeping into the East and destroying Asian values.

When the police rounded up the *boh sia* girls, some were packed off to welfare homes while others were sent back to their parents.

The girls vanished from the scene and there was silence at the Padang.

Whenever there was an important football or rugby match, a huge crowd would be at the Padang cheering the players on. Often a misdirected football would bounce onto Jalan Raja in front of Bangunan Sultan Abdul Samad and cars would screech and swerve to avoid being hit by the ball.

It was renamed Merdeka Square (Independence Square) because it was at the Padang that the Union Jack of the British colonial power was lowered and the Malayan flag raised at midnight on 30 August 1957. Some 20,000 people were there to witness the historic moment.

Just before midnight, the banks of floodlights were turned off and there was a hush as everybody turned to look at the giant clock on the tower of the government offices. When the clock started chiming at the first stroke of midnight, the lights were switched on and the police band played *God Save The Queen* as the Union Jack was lowered. Immediately after that, the band played *Negara Ku* as Tunku Abdul Rahman, who became the nation's first Prime Minister, saluted the Malayan flag which was being raised. Shouts of 'Merdeka! Merdeka!' resounded throughout Kuala Lumpur in the first few minutes of Independence Day.

New Phase, New Face

Merdeka Square has been deemed such a success that City Hall has embarked on Phase Two of the project.

This entailed the demolition of two buildings, which are old but not considered heritage buildings. These were the Malaysian Civil Servants' Sports Club and the Selangor Recreation Club, both situated in front of the Royal Selangor Club.

Being built is Kuala Lumpur's first electronic library and a gallery costing RM26 million, which will be ready in 2002. The library will have 200,000 reference books and will complement the Kuala Lumpur Memorial Library. The project was supposed to have been completed in 1998, but work began only in late 1999.

Bank of Exhibits

The former Chartered Bank building, which was constructed in 1891 at the junction of Jalan Raja and Jalan Sultan Hishamuddin, now houses the National Museum of History.

Opened in February 1996, it has sections on the pre-historic era, proto-historic era, and traces the country's history from the age of the sultanates to the modern Malaysian government. It features an interesting section on the mysterious Megalithic culture of pre-Islamic Malaya.

The star attractions are the three-storied building itself, designed by A.C. Norman, and the Dong S'on drums and bell which date from 500 B.C.

God Has Eyes

The Anglican Church
Jalan Raja

From snobs to *pondans*, this church
has seen it all.

Anglican Church

The first Anglican church was at Bluff Road and it was a timber structure which could accommodate 95 people. Built in the 1880s, it cost $1,363 with the Selangor Government contributing $500.

In 1893, it was decided that a larger church would be built and an appeal raised $5,168. The State Government topped up another $5,000.

An advertisement was published asking architects to submit plans and the new church was built in the early English Gothic style. The site at the northern end of the Padang on which the original Selangor Club had been was deemed suitable and the piece of land was levelled and planted with trees and flowers.

Since it was the era of the British Empire, the Church of England was the *de facto* official church.

The church, completed in 1894, became the place for the English settlers to socialise. It was both an expression of their identity and an expression of snobbery, given the class culture of the English at the time.

Gullick said: 'The Sunday morning service at 11 am was in the nature of a parade. The men came in top hats and long black coats. The women were in long silk or muslin dresses, with hats or bonnets, gloves and even veils. It was an occasion too in which the sense of official hierarchy found expression. The Resident was the senior member of the congregation, with a watchful eye to see whether the rank and file of the bureaucracy were all present and correct. Any junior official who absented himself for two Sundays running was likely to receive an official reproof.'

He added: 'Inside the church, a sizeable choir led the singing to the accompaniment of a harmonium. Over their heads the heavy air of the enclosed building moved sluggishly under the swish of the *punkahs*, pulled by Tamil *punkah wallahs* outside tugging on ropes.'

A century later, the church somehow attracted another kind of congregation, just as well dressed, but with different intentions. However, it was still in the nature of a parade.

Outside the church during Saturday nights in the late 1980s, *pondans* lined Jalan Raja plying their trade. Dressed in the sexiest and skimpiest of costumes, wearing wigs and high heels, they showed off their artificially-enhanced bodies, oblivious to the holy nature of the building nearby. Naturally, the gates of the church were padlocked.

Curious passers-by and potential customers gathered at the street along with hawkers selling food, drinks and cigarettes, turning the place into a jam-packed spectacle, where fun and excitement lasted till the wee hours.

There were complaints, of course—from the church council and the members of the Selangor Club. The former complained on moral grounds while the latter felt uncomfortable with such cross-dressers plying their trade right next to their posh club. It cannot be denied, however, that quite a number of the club's members strolled down the road, perhaps out of curiosity.

These times did not last.

The authorities were forced to act and police raided the place, arrested the *pondans* and chased away the unlicensed hawkers.

The situation returned to normal and the *pondans* retreated to the backlanes and cheap hotels of the city.

A CLOSER LOOK ...

At the City Centre, take the usual 'I-was-there' photographs at Merdeka Square, then head for Central Market. This is worth a visit even though many of the handicraft shops sell Balinese souvenirs and Burmese walking sticks. Outside Central Market, along J. Hang Kasturi, is the only pedestrian mall in the city. Look out for the buskers and all sorts of colourful characters here. There are lots of Indian-Muslim eateries in this area serving excellent curries. Then explore further along J. Petaling and J. Tun H.S. Lee in the direction of Chinatown where you will find a warren of stalls selling a huge variety of things including Russian binoculars, exotic food and fake Guess jeans.

The Chinatown Area

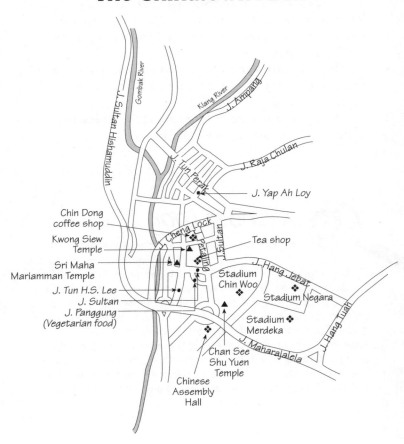

The Mother of All Markets

Jalan Petaling

Petaling Street is the Original
'Shopping Complex' of KL.

Petaling Street

I n 1895, Petaling Street during Chinese New Year was described as 'lined on each side by stalls; crowded in every conceivable crook and crannie by Chinese; two continuous lines of carriages, gharries and rickshas going in either direction; Chinese "bands" playing on the first floor of seemingly every house; a glaring sun, a blinding dust and a strong odour of cooking, etc, floated around'.

Nothing much seems to have changed, though the music these days is more likely to come from Japanese mini-compos rather than Chinese bands.

It is still crowded, though the customers are now quite multiracial, including numerous camera and camcorder-toting Caucasian and Japanese tourists. The carriages and rickshas (and even trishaws) have been replaced by Proton Sagas; but the sun is still glaring, the dust still blinds and the strong odour of cooking still lingers around.

The range of things on sale has also increased dramatically. Now, there are lots of items which would not have been available in Yap Ah Loy's time, like Russian telescopes; binoculars; watches and cameras; imitation Rolexes and Tag Heuers; fake Levi's 501 and Armani jeans; made-in-Jinjang Hard Rock Cafe and Benetton T-shirts; made-in-Cheras Gucci and Louis Vuitton bags; pirated music cassettes and VCDs.

Petaling Street was one of the first few roads to be named in Kuala Lumpur and it has retained its original name. Before 1880, there were probably only seven streets in Kuala Lumpur—Market Street, Pudoh Street, Java Street, High Street, Ampang Street, Cross Street and Petaling Street.

Petaling Street was named thus because it was the road that led to the tin mines in the Petaling area.

But the Chinese gave it a different name—Shu Chong Kai—which was Cantonese for Tapioca Factory Road. This was because Yap Ah Loy had built a tapioca mill at Petaling Street which turned the tuber into flour. In an early example of a local employing the services of a foreign consultant, the old Kapitan Cina hired an English engineer to run the mill, which had an eight-horsepower engine. It was possibly the earliest example of transfer of technology in these parts.

In the late 1870s, he had planted lots of tapioca on his land and his partner in this venture was Sultan Abdul Samad who invested $3,000.

Tapioca Mill

Yap Ah Loy also owned 12,000 acres of land along the road between Damansara and Kuala Lumpur and he had planned to plant tapioca on it. However, the tapioca venture did not take off as well as it was expected because the oxen in the plantation were killed by disease and the price of tapioca fell in 1880.

Nobody is certain when the tapioca mill closed—probably some years after the death of Yap Ah Loy in 1885—but the road is still called Shu Chong Kai by the Chinese today.

It has become famous for many things such as the longan and *loh hon kor* drink (a medicinal brew which is said to reduce the expelling of phlegm) stall in front of Hong Leong bank which does a roaring business. The proprietor has refused to move away from the awkward corner, possibly because of *feng shui*-related reasons. Nowadays, his stall is manned by a couple of Indonesian women.

The Chin Dong coffeeshop is famed for its fragrant coffee (it started out in a double-storey shophouse and when the owner amassed enough money, it was demolished to make way for a five-storey building), Koon Kee for its wantan mee and Kiew Brothers for its *nong yoke* (roast pork slices). The Ken Lian Kee shop at the corner of Petaling Street and Jalan Hang Lekir is well known for its Hokkien mee. Jalan Hang Lekir itself is known for its row of florists who used to have their stalls along the main road; now they operate from sidelanes.

Chinatown was also known for its exotic food. In the backlanes, those in the know would have their fill of what some might consider disgusting. Offered by some foodstalls were squirrel or iguana meat, turtle or anteater soup. Rumour has it that dog meat was served too.

Anteater soup anyone...

Mercedes in the Backlane

Most of the Chinese traders at Petaling Street do not appear impressive with their simple dressing and lack of ostentation, but they have Mercedes Benz cars parked in the backlanes, live in bungalows, watch satellite television and spend their holidays in Hong Kong.

A man who used to sell *kaya* (egg jam) made enough money to send his children overseas for higher education.

Petaling Street is filled with such success stories that were typical of the overseas Chinese. However, the hard-luck cases ended up begging and sleeping on five-foot ways or renting canvas beds at Petaling Street shophouses.

Business in Petaling Street is still business, though things have evolved over the years. The Swiss Inn, a quaint hotel with 110 rooms, has opened. It is connected to a few shophouses along Jalan Sultan, the road next to Petaling Street. Several budget hotels can now be found in Chinatown.

And at least two stalls with huge metal cauldrons containing herbal teas have opened selling 'cooling' concoctions and *guilinguo*, a black jelly.

The historical importance of Petaling Street and neighbouring Sultan Street has been recognised by City Hall, which has decreed that the Chinatown area will be a heritage zone and no more development projects will be approved. Chinatown will be left as it is.

Assembly of Towkays

Some of the richest Chinese towkays are represented at the Selangor Chinese Chamber of Commerce housed in the Chinese Assembly Hall, a European-styled building built in the 1920s, at the end of Petaling Street along Bulatan Merdeka.

The Chinese towkays in the early days were a fractious lot divided along dialect groups with the Cantonese and Hakkas getting at each other's throats every now and then. It took a considerable amount of diplomatic skill and a reconciliatory spirit to get all the towkays under one roof without it tumbling down on them.

The persons who worked hard to achieve unity among the towkays were Loke Yew and San Ah Wing, the latter of whom was described as 'a public spirited gentleman'.

The first meeting of the Selangor Chinese Chamber of Commerce was held on 27 March 1904, chaired by Loke Yew on neutral ground—the premises of the Selangor Miners' Association. Loke Yew, who was also chairman of the miners' association, became the first president of the chamber while San Ah Wing was its secretary. There were 20 committee members.

Loke Yew donated $50,000 towards the fund for a new building on a site that was reserved for use as a depot for immigrant coolies. Construction of the building was more problematic than expected.

The European contractor got into some difficulty and left the scene. Meanwhile, costs were rising and the Selangor Government rescinded the land title because the project was stuck. The Chinese Chamber of Commerce and the Selangor Miners' Association, afraid that they would be left out of the project, insisted on being given space in the new building.

Deciding what to name the building posed more problems. When Sun Yat Sen became a hero of the Chinese revolution against the Manchu Ching Dynasty, donors insisted on naming the building after him.

But when viceroy Chen Chiung Ming drove Sun Yat Sen out of Canton city, they had a change of heart. Chen was a Fui Chiu Hakka, the same dialect group that Yap Ah Loy belonged to.

The Hakka towkays, who still had some influence in Kuala Lumpur then, turned around and insisted that Sun Yat Sen's name should be dropped. Instead, they proposed another name for the Assembly Hall—Yap Shak Hall, after Yap Ah Loy's successor as Kapitan Cina, Yap Ah Shak.

As was normal in such disputes among the Chinese in those days, the problem was solved by the white man. Into the fray stepped the British Resident who gave the building a neutral name—Chinese Assembly Hall—and made a ruling that no bust or portrait of any Chinese towkay should be placed in it.

The hall today is used for trade fairs and exhibitions organised by people from all dialect groups.

Petaling Street started as a shopping street which was open during daylight hours. Over the years, the stalls opened for longer hours and as more people turned up for late-night shopping, the *pasar malam* came into being, with the stalls lit by kerosene pressure lamps or carbide flame lamps. Now strings of electrical light bulbs and fluorescent tubes are used.

Such *pasar malams* have become common throughout Malaysia—they are all descendants of Petaling Street.

Caring Clansmen

The herd mentality–'safety in numbers'–was the driving force behind the setting up of clan organisations among overseas Chinese communities. Starting out in a foreign land, they depended on these clan organisations for comfort, companionship and help—medical or monetary—during bad times.

One example is the Chan See Shu Yuen Temple at the end of Petaling Street—a handsome building elaborately decorated with little figurines on its walls and curved roofs. Built in 1906 to serve the Chan, Chin and Tan families, it is the oldest clan house in Kuala Lumpur and was built as a replica of the Chen Clan Classical Learning Academy in Guangzhou, China.

The clans group was set up earlier, in 1897, by tin miners and businessmen Chan Sow Lin, Chin Choon, Chin Sin Hee and Chin Choy Thin. The founders had donated seven shophouses to the temple, but construction stopped in 1902 when one of the founders died and the fortunes of the others took a dip.

In that same year, another tin miner called Chan Choy Thim made a vow during the Spring ancestral worship ceremony that he would complete the building of the temple if the gods of fortune could help him in his business. As fate would have it, he prospered and the temple was finally completed in 1906.

But apparently, the clansmen did not consult *feng shui* experts because later on, a practitioner of the art of geomancy opined that the temple was in the jaws of the white tiger, which explained the lack of success among the clansmen.

The clansmen claim that the *feng shui* changed for the better with the completion of the nearby Chin Woo stadium which has a large swimming pool, the Merdeka Stadium and the Merdeka roundabout in front of the temple which has a fountain (now disused). The swimming pool and fountain apparently symbolised wealth.

On Higher Ground

Jalan Tun H.S. Lee

*For those who ran out of luck, a rented,
foldable canvas bed awaited them along
a crowded corridor in High Street...*

The street was called High Street simply because it was on higher ground, a short walk from the swampy banks of the Klang river.

Running almost parallel to Petaling Street, High Street is one of the oldest roads in Kuala Lumpur. Like other places in this part of the city now called Chinatown, it was peopled mainly by the Chinese who set up businesses on the ground floors of their shophouses while living on the upper floors.

In some of these shophouses, the richer ones among the poor rented rooms, while those in really bad financial shape rented beds. These foldable canvas beds were placed along crowded corridors and the 'bed-tenant' slept on pillows which were made up of all of their worldly possessions wrapped in pieces of cloth.

Rioting in Chinatown

Chinatown was the scene of at least two riots.

In 1897, the *dacing* riot broke out quite suddenly. The *dacing* is a weighing instrument made up of a calibrated wooden rod and a metal pan attached to it by thick strings. The object to be weighed is placed on the pan, while a counterweight is moved up or down the rod which is suspended in the middle. The *dacing* was commonly used in the old days, but has since been replaced by modern weighing machines and electronic digital models. It is the symbol of the National Front, the political coalition which has governed Malaysia for as long as anyone can remember.

The *dacing*, like other weighing machines, can be 'adjusted' to cheat the buyer. In 1897, the police confiscated several 'adjusted' *dacing* and traders were forced to buy new ones. Only one shop had them in stock.

Word soon spread that the 'adjusted' *dacing* were confiscated to increase the business of that particular shop and an angry crowd gathered in front of it. Soon, the crowd became unruly and people started stoning the shop.

Police surrounded the crowd and it was reported that they made a bayonet charge which dispersed the angry crowd. But the gangs of people regrouped and the rioting threatened to turn uglier.

The Resident, Rodger, and an officer called H.C. Ridges rode into Chinatown and told the crowd that they would 'stand no nonsense' from the people.

In 1912, the *tauchang* riots erupted for different reasons. In 1911, the Manchu Ching Dynasty in China had been overthrown and one of the first things the reformers wanted was to discard the practice of Chinese menfolk keeping queues (pigtails) and shaving the front part of their heads. This had been made mandatory by the Manchu rulers, partly to demoralise and to ridicule the Chinese. In 1912, many Chinese in Kuala Lumpur still had their queues.

During the Chinese New Year season of 1912, tin mine workers from outstation gathered in Kuala Lumpur to shop and have some fun. 'By way of amusement, they started throwing Chinese sand-crackers into Petaling Street houses.'

Gullick continued: 'As the ribaldry increased, some of the crowd began to drag Chinese ricksha-pullers into nearby barber shops and cut off their queues. What began as a joke soon expanded into a riot which lasted a week. Old scores between different dialect and clan groups in the Chinese community flared up into open fighting.'

Rioting spread to tin mines outside Kuala Lumpur and a serious fight took place in Ampang. The police tried hard to keep things under control and the rioting soon faded away.

In the early days, High Street had a sprinkling of opium dens, gambling halls and brothels. It also had some guild halls and clansmen associations, some surviving till today. A few shops advertised in the first issue of *The Malay Mail* on 14 December 1896. These included watch and clock maker, Yee Woh at No. 93; and Siew Sang at No. 48, which dealt in Japanese curios.

While many rich Chinese towkays had Jalan Ampang residences, Kapitan Cina Yap Kwan Seng lived at High Street on the site of today's Lee Rubber Building.

Over the years, High Street evolved and its name was changed to Jalan Bandar and later Jalan Tun H.S. Lee, in honour of a founding father of this nation.

Businesses have changed hands and some modern buildings have replaced old ones, but Jalan Tun H.S. Lee today still bears some resemblance to the High Street of ancient times.

In the early part of the 20th century, the section of High Street near Yap Ah Loy Street was called Ng Chee Tang ('five lanterns' in Cantonese) because there were five oil street lamps at a small square in the middle of the road. Until around 1885, coconut oil was used as fuel for street lamps. That same year, the oil lamps on wooden posts were replaced by kerosene lamps on iron posts.

For some reason, this area attracted goldsmiths. Even today, that section has a row of goldsmiths which brings in huge crowds. Seated outside these shops are guards, mostly ex-servicemen, armed with shotguns.

Goldsmiths galore ...

The road also has several shops selling crockery—porcelain plates, bowls, vases, urns, cups and tea sets. Near its junction with Jalan Cheng Lock is the Hong Leong Building, behind which is the Sin Sze Si Ya Temple built by Yap Ah Loy.

Further along the road near its junction with Jalan Hang Lekir are two popular tourist destinations—the Kwong Siew Temple and opposite it, the Sri Maha Mariamman Temple, where the Silver Chariot used for the procession of Murugan to Batu Caves during Thaipusam is kept.

The Temple of Boom

The story of the Sri Maha Mariamman Temple is connected to that of Thamboosamy Pillai, the richest and most influential Indian in the Kuala Lumpur of his time.

Thamboosamy Pillai was born around 1850 in Singapore and studied at Raffles Institution. After his education, he worked as a legal clerk for a Singaporean law firm.

When a partner of the firm, Mr J.G. Davidson, was sent to Selangor in 1875 to take up the post as the first British Resident. His able assistant, Thamboosamy Pillai, tagged along. Pillai later became the chief clerk in the Treasury and left the civil service in 1889 to try his hand in business. Tin mining in Rawang was his first venture, and it is for that mine and the electricity it introduced to Malaya that he is remembered till today, along with his partner Loke Yew.

As his fortune grew, he built the road from Kuala Lumpur to Rawang and further on to Kuala Kubu Baru. Loke Yew, perhaps the richest man in Malaya then, was his partner in several ventures.

He also developed coffee estates in the vicinity of Klang and became owner of much property at Java Street, the popular shopping area of town. Thamboosamy Pillai died in 1902, but he left a legacy that is still important to the city today.

Robson described him as someone who 'knew everybody and was known to everybody... a leading light in Selangor Club... almost an institution in himself... keenly interested in racing, and a curry tiffin at his house on the Batu Road was something to remember'.

One of his most important legacies is the Sri Maha Mariamman Temple. Founded in 1873 and originally sited somewhere near the railway station, it was relocated to High Street in 1885. The original attap structure was demolished in 1887 and a brick building was erected. That structure was demolished in 1964.

The existing buildings date from 1965. The impressive *gopuram* (gateway) was built in 1972 and the temple building dates from 1968.

Mariamman was popularly worshipped by overseas Indians, especially Tamils, because it was looked upon as their protector during their sojourn in foreign lands.

Sri Maha Mariamman Temple is not only the oldest temple in Malaysia but also the richest. A 1986 report had it that it owned shops, gold and land worth about $20–$30 million. It had an annual income of $2 million from donations, rentals and payments for temple services.

It is one of the most important temples in Kuala Lumpur because every Thaipusam, the Silver Chariot with the statuettes of Murugan and his consorts—Valli and Teivayanni—leaves its gates at around 4 am. Pulled by white bullocks, it makes its way to the Batu Caves. Usually, a large crowd will wait outside the temple from as early as 3 am and when the huge gates open, musicians and drummers will break into song and the crowd will start chanting at the sight of the brightly-lit chariot.

The management committee which runs the Sri Maha Mariamman Temple also supervises the Subramaniam Temple in the Batu Caves and the Sri Vinayagar Temple at Court Hill (where the Maybank tower is sited) near Jalan Pudu Lama.

Chariot of the Gods

The Silver Chariot bearing the idol of Murugan and his consorts, that is used for the Thaipusam procession annually, made its debut in 1983. It was built at a cost of $350,000 using 350 kilogrammes of silver.

The chariot was made in India and shipped here in 12 parts to be assembled. A team of carpenters and craftsmen from India were in Kuala Lumpur for several months to get it in shape. It is 6.5 metres tall, and has 240 bells and a pair of horses on it.

Before the Silver Chariot, a wooden one was used which was made in 1930 by Indian craftsmen at a cost of $50,000.

Kwong Siew Temple

The Kwong Siew Temple, built in 1888 and managed by the Kwong Siew Association, was recently refurbished.

At the junction of Jalan Tun H.S. Lee and Jalan Sultan is one of Kuala Lumpur's few conservation projects. A row of prewar shophouses has been converted into a modern shopping complex—the UDA-Ocean shopping centre. Opposite it is another conservation project which is an extension of the shopping centre and the two projects are linked by an aerial bridge.

Jalan Tun H.S. Lee ends somewhere near the traffic police headquarters and the old High Street police station. Next to the traffic police headquarters is the original Victoria Institution which was recently damaged in a fire.

Helluva Hazard

The Selangor Golf Club
Jalan Hang Jebat

Golf in Malaysia was born in a graveyard.

When you fly into Kuala Lumpur at night, you might see two spots which are brightly lit near the Sultan Abdul Aziz international airport (formerly known as the Subang airport).

You might think these are gigantic industrial complexes powering the nation's relentless drive towards industrialisation.

Far from it—the only driving done in these brightly-lit areas is by Big Berthas or Killer Bees.

Night golfing may be bad news to pilots, but it is good news to those adventurous enough to play golf after dusk and to Tenaga Nasional, the national power producer.

Golf in Malaysia is now a booming industry attracting Singaporeans and Japanese by the thousands. The game has also 'greened' many areas which used to look more like deserts after tin mining had depleted them of vegetation.

Not only the living, but the dead had to make way for the game of golf. The first golf course in Malaya was built on an ancient Chinese graveyard on Petaling Hill, smack in the midst of Kuala Lumpur's Chinatown in 1893.

Bounded by Davidson Road (now called Jalan Hang Jebat), Shaw Road (Jalan Hang Tuah) and Birch Road (Jalan Maharajalela) the graveyard was converted into a golf course for the pleasure of the colonialists while the Chinamen probably looked on with a mixture of astonishment and bewilderment as the white masters sipped *stengahs*, swung clubs at little balls and swore when they missed their putts. What a waste of time, the early Chinamen must have thought, but as is evident now, things have changed a lot.

With names like Swettenham, Venning, Syers, Hose, Spooner, Treacher, Young and Brockman gracing the portal of the Selangor Golf Club, the nearest any Chinaman got to hobnobbing with such esteemed company then was probably as a waiter serving tea and tiffin.

Skullduggery Along the Fairway

The caddies were Malays mainly because the Chinese would rather not disturb the spirits which they feared could still be lurking in the former graveyard. Most of the skeletons however, had been disinterred and sent to China for reburial. According to Gullick, 'the firm rather than scientific use of a niblick in the remoter parts of the rough would occasionally unearth a bone or a skull'.

Unearthing a bone or a skull ...

Golf was a white man's game and it was only some 16 years after the club opened that a handful of Asians became members. One of the first was Towkay Choo Kia Peng.

The club was officially opened on 21 August 1893 with 30 members and the original clubhouse was a far cry from the imposing splendour of today's—it was a tent. A rich donor later gave money for a pavilion and a horse shed to be built.

According to Gullick, the pavilion was at the base of the hill and was moved in 1895 to make way for an incinerator. Golfers teed off beside the clubhouse, which was located near today's Rumah Baden Powell, and the course layout had the fairway heading towards where Stadium Negara is now located, up to the former Tunku Abdul Rahman Park and down the hill back to the clubhouse.

The initiative to start the Selangor Golf Club began with an announcement in the 13 January 1893 issue of the *Selangor Journal* that read: 'A meeting will be held at the Selangor Club on Sat, the 21st inst., at 6 p.m. to consider the advisability of forming a golf club in Kuala Lumpur. All interested are invited to attend.'

The drivers behind that were the brothers Clem and John Glassford, who owned a coffee plantation at Mount Estate, Bentong Road, and Kit and Robert Meikle. 30 members of the European community attended that meeting.

The Glassford brothers and Mr. A.T.D. Berrington, Chief Magistrate of Selangor, proceeded to lay the course over former graves and they estimated the cost of 'preparing the links and getting them in order for one year' to be $300. Nine holes were laid in time for the opening. Rather aptly, one hazard was called 'Hell'—it was a deep ravine from which no mishit ball could be retrieved and given that the course was on a former graveyard, nobody would risk getting the ball back anyway.

Those days, the golfers were a gracious lot and women were also allowed to play. In fact, a prize was offered for a ladies' handicap in 1896.

The British planters, miners and administrators had a wonderful time teeing off and sipping tea till after World War I, when the government decided to acquire the course to turn it into a public park.

Second Oldest in Asia

However, the government provided an alternative piece of land and financed the construction of an 18-hole course plus a proper clubhouse at Circular Road (now called Jalan Tun Razak). That club, which opened in 1921, is now called the Royal Selangor Golf Club and it has 36 holes. It holds the distinction of being the second oldest premier golf club in Asia after the Royal Calcutta.

The park at Petaling Hill was later renamed after the first Malaysian Prime Minister, Tunku Abdul Rahman.

RSCG—A Royal Birdie

The Royal Selangor Golf Club at Jalan Langgak Golf, off Jalan Tun Razak, is the mother of golf clubs in Malaysia and was conferred the royal title in 1963. It was then the best club around.

But during the Japanese Occupation, it was in bad shape with its greens overgrown with weeds, fairways dug up and trees felled. The Japanese invaders—who at that time wielded samurai swords instead of Mizuno clubs—occupied the course and built barracks for their troops.

Trees along the fairways were chopped down and wells dug while troops overran the clubhouse. And believe it or not, a landing strip for airplanes was constructed at the course.

The locals lived in squatter huts in other parts of the course and grew vegetables, tapioca and bananas for food because rice was in short supply.

After the war ended, it took almost three years to rehabilitate the course and it reopened in March 1948. The credit for reopening the course goes to Tom Verity, who resumed his duty as the club pro after the war.

Five years later, the four nine-hole courses were combined to form the Old Course which measures 6,328 metres and the New Course measuring 5,921 metres. Both are par-72 courses.

The RSGC, as it is commonly called, is on 146 hectares of land. When the Government decided to close the original course at Petaling Hill and offer the land at Circular Road, the site was being partly occupied by tin miners and a Forestry Department research station. The miners left after being persuaded to do so by Towkay Choo and compensated by the authorities, while the Forestry Department left behind the majestic tembusu trees still standing today.

From Jalan Hang Jebat, there is a staircase that leads to the park. This is the much-dreaded staircase that students of Victoria Institution had to climb every morning to get to the school nearby. It is reputed to be the second longest staircase in Malaysia, after the one at Batu Caves.

Many years ago, a rock landscape made of cement was built and it served as a popular backdrop for wedding shots. It was also a popular spot for certain other premarital activities.

In the vicinity are the Chin Woo auditorium, which boasts one of the largest swimming pools in Kuala Lumpur, an open area called Changkat Pavilion which was used for trade fairs and exhibitions, and two of the most important landmarks in the city—the Merdeka and Negara stadia.

A grandson of Yap Ah Loy, Mr George Yap Swee Fatt, 83, was quoted in 1993 as saying that he used to live in a mansion on 15 acres of land where the Chin Woo stadium now stands.

He recalled the greens of the Selangor Golf Club which he passed daily on his way to school at Victoria Institution.

Malaysia now has about 200 golf courses, many of which have been laid out by some of the world's best course designers. There are about 60,000 registered golfers. Not bad for a game started by 30 Europeans.

Last Hurrah for Stadia

Merdeka Stadium and Stadium Negara
Jalan Stadium

*The arena in which an unforgettable moment
in Malaysia's history took place becomes
yet another memory.*

Every Malaysian will remember the familiar photograph of the Father of the Nation, Tunku Abdul Rahman, with his right hand raised as he shouted 'Merdeka' seven times. It is an image that has been used so frequently and in so many forms that it is eternally etched in the psyche of Malaysians. Indeed, it has become the image of independence.

That memorable moment was enacted on 31 August 1957 at Merdeka Stadium, which was completed just in time for the Independence celebrations.

On that day, Tunku Abdul Rahman wore a black Malay tunic called *baju maskat*, which was worn by civil servants in Kedah during the reign of Sultan Abdul Hamid (1882–1943). Tunku was a proud man that day as he had led a nation to independence without bloodshed. When he shouted 'Merdeka', the entire stadium, filled to its brim with tens of thousands of jubilant people, resounded with the word that held so much meaning for them.

Independence without bloodshed ...

Stadium Merdeka, which was the largest project in Malaya at that time, became a memory when it was closed after the Commonwealth Games in September 1998.

A company called UEM was given the right to redevelop the stadium plus neighbouring Stadium Negara, Changkat Pavilion (a disused trade fair venue) and Tunku Abdul Rahman Park (the second oldest park in the city).

The 12.8 hectare site, situated where Kuala Lumpur's first golf course was located, will be redeveloped into condos, retail outlets, shopping complexes and entertainment shops.

In exchange for the development right, UEM teamed up with Ho Hup to build the RM700 million National Sports Complex on 61.2 hectares of land in Bukit Jalil, at the outskirts of Kuala Lumpur, creating a Games Village complete with accommodation for athletes and officials and venues for various events.

The consortium also built the main stadium, an indoor stadium, an aquatic complex, squash courts and hockey stadium.

Sunny Side Still Up

In between the two stadia along Jalan Stadium was an eatery nicknamed 'mushroom' after its supposed shape.

Behind the 'mushroom' was a sun dial that was bowl-like and crescent shaped. It served a dual function — it told time quite accurately, and children used it as a slide.

The Merdeka Sun Clock, as it was called, was built by the same Public Works Department engineer who designed Stadium Negara, S.E. Jewkes, who enlisted the help of his colleague Chan Sai Soo. It was given that name because it was built to commemorate independence in 1957.

'This sun dial is of an unusual type and is the first of its kind in the world. Chan and I worked out the mathematical details to ensure that the sun dial gives the correct time and month,' Jewkes was reported as saying.

The sun dial had mosaic tiles and the shadow of an 11-point star fixed to the wall of the 'mushroom' fell on numbers and Zodiac figures, telling the time and month.

Due to the redevelopment of Stadium Negara and Merdeka, the Merdeka Sun Clock was removed.

Its new home is the National Planetarium near the Lake Gardens.

But not every facet of history will be lost because the Heritage Plaza, which will highlight the historical significance of Stadium Merdeka, will be built for the sake of future generations of Malaysians. According to the original plans, People's Park, incorporating the existing Tunku Abdul Rahman Park, will also be part of the project.

Stadium Negara, which was built in 1962 at a cost of RM1.5 million, had the largest unsupported roof in the region. Designed by Public Works Department engineer S.E. Jewkes, the indoor stadium could seat 10,200. The roof, which developed leaks, was replaced with a space-frame dome in 1985.

Stadium Negara has seen numerous sporting events, such as thrilling Thomas Cup badminton matches. It has also been the venue of concerts by the Osmonds, Boney M, Eric Clapton, Tina Turner, Air Supply and others despite its inadequate acoustics. Today, with newer venues available, Stadium Negara has lost its appeal.

The two stadia, which are landmarks in the city, are in their last lap. When the redevelopment project takes off, they will probably be reduced to rubble.

A CLOSER LOOK ...

At Chinatown, take your time to browse around. In some dusty corner of an old forgotten mom-and-pop cubicle you can often find something really interesting, although the fast-selling fake designer jeans and Rolex watches have been moved to the front shelves. I often pop into a shop selling Chinese tea and tea pots (at the junction of J. Sultan and J. Petaling) and just have a look at the cute designs or buy some tea. Then I walk to one of those herbal drink shops and have *guilingao* (a kind of black jelly) or pop into Chin Dong coffeeshop (along J. Petaling) for a cup of its famous coffee. I used to have late-night suppers at the stall selling Hokkien mee (opposite Chin Dong coffeeshop). Sometimes I also have Chinese vegetarian meals at the shops along J. Panggung.

Jalan Ampang Area

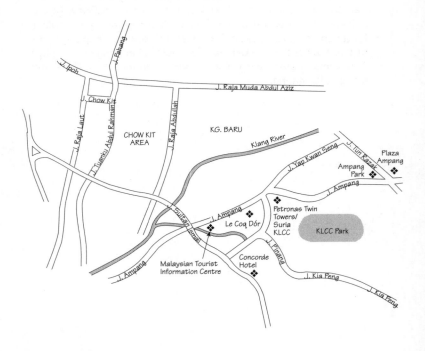

Nightmare Turns Into Sweet Dream

Selangor Turf Club
Jalan Ampang

Fortunes are made and lost at the turf club...

It started with a Nightmare and ended, 96 years later, with a Sweet Dream—that unlikely turn of events was indeed the story of the Selangor Turf Club (STC).

The first race at the STC was held in March 1896 and it was won by an amateur rider Paton Ker who rode Nightmare to a dream victory. When the last race events were held on 23 August 1992, punters were pleasantly surprised by the special RM70,000 stake for the 1,900-metre fifth race called Farewell and Sweet Dream Stakes.

That special race, sponsored by mattress manufacturer Sweet Dream Industrial Corporation Sdn Bhd, was won by Paul Harvey, a visiting jockey, on Miraculous.

Some 20,000 punters turned up for the final races at the STC, some to make (or lose) money as they had habitually done for years, and others to bid farewell to The Old Lady (old-timers gave it that sobriquet) before it was demolished to make way for the Kuala Lumpur City Centre project.

They were given a Big Sweep lottery ticket and a pen each by the STC as souvenirs. The final races, called the Ampang Farewell Stakes, was a touching affair—the popular disco song *The Final Countdown* was played over the PA system before the eighth race and when the evening came to an end, 9,600 red and yellow balloons, the colours of the STC, were released and *Auld Lang Syne* was sung. Some tears were shed. Those who bet on the wrong horses shed even more tears.

The last race at The Old Lady was won by jockey Foo Yung Kong riding Superior Being in a time of 1 minute 52.5 seconds. It paid RM59 for a win and RM24 for a place.

Then, the curtains came down on the track and the bulldozers moved in.

In March 1896, the first races at the Ampang Road Turf Club were held over two days featuring seven events per day.

Horse racing however, had reached Selangor several years before that. In February 1890, a Gymkhana Club was formed with some Chinese members and Towkay Ah Yeok was a member of the first committee. Towkay Loke Yew was among the list of horse owners. While horse racing was starting to be organised in Selangor, there were already full-fledged turf clubs in Singapore and Penang.

The Gymkhana Club asked the Selangor Government for a five-year lease of land at the Rifle Range Road, in the Circular Road (now called Jalan Tun Razak) area, for a course.

The lease was granted along with a subsidy of $2,000 which was used together with $1,500 contributed by the members for laying the course.

Quite aptly, the first race was held in 1891 during Chinese New Year, in conjunction with a visit by the Governor. For a bit of comic relief, an obstacle race was included where the jockeys had to carry unopened umbrellas and light up cigars before mounting their horses.

The next year, a brick grandstand, which could seat 250 people, was built and one or two races were held annually after that.

However, KL races failed to attract entries from outside Selangor because a stipulation in the lease prevented the Gymkhana Club from allowing professional jockeys to participate in its races. One of the better amateur jockeys was police chief Syers.

When the lease expired in 1895, the set-up was reorganised and in September that year, the Gymkhana Club was wound up and relaunched as the Selangor Turf Club. Its committee immediately started negotiations with the Selangor Government for a lease of a new course without restriction on the admission of professional jockeys.

In the old days, turning up at the races was a social event and, next to the Selangor Club and Lake Club, it was the place for women to be seen wearing the latest sartorial styles and hats from London. The values of that time dictated that women should be seen as fashionable, definitely not as gamblers.

Fashion at the Paddocks

Gullick described the situation thus: 'Much of the fun of race meetings, as always, lay in backing your fancy. This presented some nice problems to a late Victorian community which had no bookmakers among its numbers and which did not feel quite easy about its women betting (smoking, riding bicycles, etc). The Chartered Bank solved the first of these problems by making a practice of closing on race days and bringing its cashiers out to the course to constitute the Old Firm. One of the stewards was deputed to collect the ladies' bets and place them; thus the proprieties were saved. There was something in the nature of a dress parade after the last race in the enclosure.'

Gullick added that 'class distinctions were not forgotten. The nobs occupied the "club stand" and the *hoi polloi* viewed the races from the "native stand".'

The major events then were the Miner's Purse worth a princely sum of $1,000 and the Resident's Cup worth $250. The latter was limited to Australian yearling horses, or griffins, which were horses that had not raced before

Taking part in the events were ponies from Burma, Java, Sumatra and China. These were replaced much later by thoroughbreds from Australia and New Zealand.

Locally-bred horses started participating only as recently as 1974. Now, the horses are from England, France, America and Ireland.

In the first year, the Selangor Turf Club had 110 members and since then, luminaries from Malaysia's past such as Loke Yew, Tun Sir H.S. Lee, Datuk Clough Thuraisingam and Dr E.A.O. Travers have featured prominently in the horse-racing scene. During the early years, the committee was a white domain and non-whites were allowed to join only in 1947.

The STC's quaint attap-roofed pavilion was replaced with a $1-million concrete structure in 1956 and the Royal Stand was opened by the first Malaysian Prime Minister, Tunku Abdul Rahman, in 1966. The Royal Stand had been graced by many a dignitary, but the most elegant was Queen Elizabeth II, who was at the races on 15 October 1989 when she visited Malaysia for a Commonwealth Heads of Government meeting.

As an increasing number of people turned up at the races in a mad rush to win princely fortunes, the narrow roads leading to the race course, which was situated in the middle of the Central Business District, became more and more congested.

Each year saw only 24 on-course races, but there were 80 off-course races which were events held in other cities and towns but were telecast live at the Jalan Ampang Turf Club. Punters, being the hardcore gamblers they were, still turned up to watch the outstation races on television. It was quite comical to watch them screaming and shouting at TV sets. Even when there were no races at the Jalan Ampang Turf Club, there were still massive traffic jams.

Not only were fortunes lost, but man-hours and productivity too. Public outcry crescendoed, forcing the government to **Public outcry crescendoed ...** step in and make a decision to shift the race course. By 1985, a temporary off-course betting centre was in operation in Sungei Besi. In 1988, the STC was given notice to shift within three years.

A site opposite the temporary off-course betting centre was selected and an international-class course was built on 256 acres of land. It had a grandstand which could seat 15,000 people, paddocks, equine pools and stables. And not to forget, 250 tote counters.

The first race at the new turf club beside the Seremban Highway was held in October 1993. Did the fact that the new course was rather far from the city bother the horse-racing *kakis* (gang)? 'No problem-lah,' they said.

Now, residents of that area are complaining about traffic jams. One just can't win them all.

The Golden Age of the
Golden Rooster

Le Coq D'or

Jalan Ampang

*How did a bicycle seller win over the
daughter of a rich towkay?*

L e Coq D'or, one of the oldest restaurants in Kuala Lumpur, is housed in one of the most palatial homes in the city.

The restaurant occupies one wing of the Bok House and it is the kind of place that resonates with history. It even smells old.

At the lobby, neoclassical marble statues are placed next to antique Chinese black wood furniture with inlaid mother-of-pearl, including an opium bed.

The staircase has cast iron railings in the Art Nouveau style. On the rear wall of the main building, stained glass windows feature hunting scenes. Old oil paintings line the walls.

Just like Loke Yew, the owner of the mansion, Chua Cheng Bok, was a well-travelled man, and he had cosmopolitan values which were reflected in the grand old mansion he built on the road that led to the Ampang tin mines.

In the old days, stately mansions lined the road. That was where the rich Chinese miners and traders shifted to, while the Europeans lived along the Damansara road.

Now, only a few mansions are left and skyscrapers have sprouted around them as land value in that area skyrocketed in recent times.

Chua started out selling bicycles and ended up selling Mercedes Benz luxury cars. Talk about upward mobility in the old days...

From bicycles to Mercedes Benzes ...

He made a massive fortune and the company he founded with his brother, Cheng Liat, in August 1899—Cycle and

Carriage Company—is still listed on the Stock Exchanges of Kuala Lumpur and Singapore. Initially, Cycle and Carriage was a grocery store and it expanded into a haberdashery selling perfumes, hats, guns, soaps, shoes, golf clubs and cigars. Later it sold bicycles and offered carriage repair, painting and varnishing services.

By the first decade of the 20th century, it had forged links with automobile companies and became the exclusive dealer for European car manufacturers, especially Daimler Benz AG.

Cycle and Carriage imported some of the first cars to Malaysia and even today, selling cars—Mercedes Benz, Isuzu and Mitsubishi (and Protons in Singapore)—is still its core business, though it has diversified into property development.

Love Story

Apparently, Chua Cheng Bok had fallen in love with a daughter of Towkay Choo Kia Peng, but the towkay had looked down on Chua, the bicycle seller. When Chua made it to the big league, he built his mansion in 1929 on a specially-chosen site—directly opposite Towkay Choo's house.

Singaporean architects Swan and Maclaren were commissioned to design the house in a Renaissance style with a local influence. The love story has a romantic ending. With the one-upmanship, Towkay Choo was impressed enough to approve the marriage of his daughter to tycoon Chua.

The Bok House is still intact today thanks to a trust set up by Chua. The trust states that the stately home is to remain as it is for 40 years after the death of Mrs Chua after which it is to be used to provide education to poor Chinese children. Without this trust, Kuala Lumpur's architectural heritage would have been much poorer. It has also ensured that all the artifacts bought by the Chua family such as the Roman statues, black wood Chinese furniture, chandeliers, brass lions and European oil paintings have remained as they are, probably even in their original positions.

Bok House

The Bok House actually comprises two houses and servants' quarters. While Le Coq D'or (French for 'The Golden Rooster') operated from the front house, Mrs Chua lived in the house behind till her death in the 1960s. During the Japanese Occupation, the Yokohama Specie Bank occupied the front of the mansion from 1943 to 1944.

Le Coq D'or, which started business in 1958, had its glory days when the British were still serving in the newly-independent Malaya. Planters, miners, businessmen and London-trained natives turned up for their meals. Some simply walked over from the nearby Selangor Turf Club with wallets fattened with winnings for a dinner treat.

A trio played soft music while the diners had their fill of chicken in coconut soup (a curry with herbs), which is a speciality, and steaks. For dessert, there was Peach Melba or Bomb Alaska.

Christmas and New Year's Eve were gala occasions when men in smart tuxedos and women in shimmering evening dresses turned up to wine and dine. Guests spilled over to the lobby, where they danced next to the Roman statues beneath the crystal chandelier and strings of colourful light bulbs. The ladies caught their breath on the black wood chairs and powdered their noses at the quaint WC upstairs.

On other days, a pianist played at the lobby. Private parties were held at the large balcony upstairs overlooking Ampang Road.

But all the partying had to end at around midnight because Mrs Chua, who lived just behind, found it too noisy.

These days, there are other popular restaurants in Kuala Lumpur serving excellent Continental cuisine. But none of them has the romantic aura or the golden past of Le Coq D'or.

The Taller You Are, the Harder You Fall

Petronas Towers

Jalan Ampang

*The never-ending battle to be the
world's tallest continues...*

There never was a tussle over the title of 'Tallest Building in the World' in the old days. Everyone knew it was the Empire State Building in New York. Nobody questioned that.

Then that was overtaken by the World Trade Centre in Manhattan and later by the Sears Tower in Chicago. When news arrived that Malaysia was challenging the Sears Tower's record position at the top of the world, chaos ensued.

The drama unfolded when an eight-member committee of the Council on Tall Buildings and Urban Habitat unanimously voted for Petronas (Petroliam Nasional or National Petroleum Corporation) Towers to be the tallest building in the world in the early part of 1996.

That sparked off a debate which was extensively covered by the print and television media in the United States. The problem was a simple question of whether a pinnacle or a television broadcasting tower should be included as part of a building.

According to the rules of the Council on Tall Buildings and Urban Habitat, set up in 1969 and comprising architects, engineers and planners, the height of a building should be measured from the front entrance of the ground floor up to the structural top. Thus flagpoles and TV antennae do not count but decorative spires, or pinnacles, do. In this way, Petronas Towers topped Sears Tower by a pinnacle.

The Petronas Towers are 378 metres from the ground floor to the top of the highest occupied floor. With the stainless steel pinnacles, the towers stand at 452 metres—10 metres taller than Sears Tower.

'Tall tale!' cried the Chicago authorities who called foul play. The Sears Tower has 110 storeys while the Petronas Towers have only 88. They alleged that the Malaysians added the needle-like pinnacles just to spite the Americans.

Petronas Towers

They proposed a new way to measure a building's height called the 'hats off' definition, which means a building must be measured without decorative hats—from the ground floor to the roof of the last functional floor. Sears Tower has a flat roof which is 442 metres from street level.

The Chicago authorities also tendered a second argument —that the two 20-metre long steel tubes on top of the building, which act as TV broadcast antennae, should be considered as part of the building's structure. With that extra bit, Sears Tower would measure 462 metres and retain the title of World's Tallest Building by 10 metres.

Rather conveniently, they did not even mention that if TV antennae were to be considered part of a building's structure, the World's Tallest Building would then be the World Trade Centre in New York, which is also crowned with TV antennae. If these were to be added to the buildings' height, it would set a new record of 527 metres.

Ironically, the Sears Tower, completed in 1974, had snatched the title from the World Trade Centre in the first place. The World Trade Centre comprising twin towers measuring 417 metres and 415 metres had been completed just one year earlier.

Furthermore, the engineer involved in the building of the Sears Tower, the late Fazlun Khan, who worked for architect firm Skidmore, Owings & Merrill, was involved in formulating the existing definition of a building's height when he was a member of the Council on Tall Buildings and Urban Habitat, the very same council which ruled that Petronas Towers were the new champions. And Fazlun Khan had always stated that Sears Tower measured 441 metres.

'It Feels Taller...'

A spokesman for the Chicago Department of Planning and Development was reported as saying: 'Any Chicagon worth their salt and with their pride believes we still have the tallest building.'

Mr Gerald Johnson, chairman of the Chicago Committee on Highrise Buildings, was reported as saying: 'It looks taller, it feels taller, it is taller. The Sears Tower remains the tallest building you or I will ever stand on.'

John Buck Co, which runs the Sears Tower, will continue to tell visitors on its observatory deck that they are on the tallest building in the world.

In Malaysia, visitors to the Petronas Towers will also be told that they are on the tallest buildings in the world.

Both parties will be wasting their time and energy because all that brouhaha is destined to be an exercise in futility anyway. By 2002, the World's Tallest Building title will be snatched from Petronas Towers by the 460-metre 94-storied Shanghai World Financial Centre Tower in China, which is already under construction. However, this building in Shanghai will hold the title of the world's tallest only for a while because Australian property developer Bruno Grollo recently announced plans to build a 560-metre 113-storied Grollo Tower in Melbourne. Costing A\$1.5 billion, it will be twice the height of Australia's present tallest building, the 55-storied Rialto Tower in the same city, which was also built by Grollo. But the Grollo Tower could end up as a non-starter because of opposition from residents and the authorities.

All this haggling is not new. Owners of the Chrysler building had haggled with the owners of the Empire State Building for that honour when the latter building was completed in 1931. The Empire State Building on Fifth Avenue, New York, had measured 381 metres while the Chrysler building was 319 metres tall. When a television mast was added in 1951, the Empire State Building's height reached 449 metres—the undisputed world champion until the World Trade Centre was completed in 1973.

The Americans had always held that title from the time the Woolworth building in New York, measuring 241 metres, was erected in 1913. Sixty of the world's 100 tallest buildings are in the United States, with three of the 10 tallest in Chicago and another three in New York.

Seen in this light, it is understandable that the Americans are highly reluctant to pass on the title to someone else. It would not be surprising if an American will someday build a mega-skyscraper so tall that no brash upstart from a remote corner of the world would surpass for a long, long time.

True enough, in August 1996, renowned developer Donald Trump unveiled his plans to build a 546-metre 140-storied skyscraper and proposed the project to the New York Stock Exchange which is seeking a new headquarters.

It looked like the Big Apple was to have the last bite until its rival Chicago snatched the prize away from the New Yorkers.

While nothing more has been heard from Trump, other than news that he will end up owning the Empire State Building, a group of businessmen from Chicago proposed to build a 468-metre 112-storied building in June 1999.

Contenders from other parts of the world include—the Citygate Ecotower in London (460 metres, 108 floors), the Sao Paulo Tower in Brazil (495 metres, 105 floors) and the Landmark Tower in Hong Kong (574 metres, 97 floors).

While these projects are awaiting approval, the Petronas Twin Towers, officially launched on 31 August 1999 in conjunction with Malaysia's 42nd National Day, remain the tallest buildings in the world, at least for another year or two.

The Making of Petronas Towers

In March 1996, the Petronas Towers at Jalan Ampang were crowned with the controversial 73.5-metre stainless steel pinnacles which officially made the buildings the world's tallest—and sparked off a passionate debate half way across the world on whether the previous holder of that title, the Sears Tower in Chicago, should relinquish the honour.

With the pinnacles, the Petronas Towers stand at 452 metres surpassing Sears Tower by 10 metres. The pinnacles feature aviation lights and facilities for cleaning the exterior cladding of the upper floors.

Prime mover of the project, Prime Minister Datuk Seri Dr Mahathir Mohamad had the honour of topping-up the building on 13 February 1996.

The multi-billion-ringgit Petronas Towers are built on a site where punters made and lost fortunes on horse racing. The Selangor Turf Club was the venue for thousands of would-be millionaires every race day and many tall buildings in the vicinity were designed in such a way that they would have a good view of the race course. For example, the Kuala Lumpur Hilton had a restaurant-cum-bar called the Paddock on the 30th floor where punters could chat over tea and sandwiches while watching the races through binoculars. In the true spirit of betting, the Selangor Turf Club has wagered on the success of the billion-ringgit KL City Centre (of which the Petronas Towers are a part) and it has some equity in the project.

Initially, there was a proposal to build a park at the Turf Club site, but the businessmen overruled the greenies. A move that is not too difficult to understand given that land in that area—smack in the middle of the Central Business District—was worth more than a gram of gold per square metre. The mega-project, the largest in Malaysia and one of the largest in the world, was given the green light, but there was some compromise—the number of floors was increased so that there could be space for a park, albeit smaller than originally envisioned.

Unique Skybridge

Petronas scored some corporate-image-building points when it spent a small fortune removing 200 mature trees, roots and all, from around the turf club to a special nursery where they were nurtured till they could be replanted in the park.

Renowned designer Roberto Burle Marx, the master of gardens from Brazil, was hired to plan the park, but he did not live to see it to fruition. Already 80 when engaged for the project, he passed away in 1994. But he had drafted plans for an urban park with streams, fountains, waterfalls, floral paths and manicured gardens on about 20 hectares of land.

An international contest for the master plan was held and the winning entry was from the American firm Klages, Carter, Vail and Associates who recommended development around the perimeter of the park.

A New York-based architect, the renowned Cesar Pelli, winner of the American Institute of Architects Gold Medal, designed the towers and he included the unique feature of a skybridge connecting the two towers on the 41st and 42nd floors.

Contractors from all over the world took part in the bid for the project. Japanese and South Korean firms formed joint ventures with Malaysians to build the structures. When building the substructure, a record was set in December 1993 when cement was poured continuously for the raft foundation of Tower One. Some 13,200 cubic metres of Grade 60 concrete weighing about 32,350 tonnes was poured continuously for 54 hours into the site, making it the largest single concrete pour in the world. The raft foundations support the buildings which weigh 270,000 tonnes. The sophisticated foundation comprises 4.5 metre-thick piled raft 20 metres below ground supported by 104 friction piles ranging in depth from 40 to 105 metres. They can take 2.5 times the weight of the building.

In an ironic twist, engineering consultants **An ironic** from Chicago were hired for a second opinion **twist ...** on the design specifications of the foundation.

There were some problems encountered even before construction began. Soil tests confirmed that the original site was on limestone with cavities and the entire project had to be shifted 50 metres south where there was solid bedrock.

The newly-constructed towers are part of KL City Centre which include a 50-storeyed Esso Tower to house the oil company's headquarters, a 628-roomed Mandarin Hotel (which will have the largest ballroom in Malaysia) and a shopping mall with three anchor tenants—Isetan (its largest store in Malaysia), Parkson and Marks & Spencer. In later phases, more skyscrapers will be built around the perimeter of the park.

Other than the fact that they are the tallest buildings in the world, the Petronas Towers hold another record—they have the largest number of double-decker elevators in the world with 29 in each tower. Made by Otis, they are also the first double-decker lifts in Malaysia.

Urban Kampung

Kampung Baru

*Between Jalan Raja Abdullah
and Jalan Raja Muda*

Untouched by the frantic pace of the city,
things have remained constant in this village.

A river separates the rich from the poor. On one side of
the Klang river along Jalan Ampang and Jalan Yap Kwan
Seng, there are still a few fabulous mansions belonging to old-
monied Chinese and numerous skyscrapers built on land that
is more valuable than gold. Not surprisingly, the area around
Jalan Ampang is called The Golden Triangle.

On the other side of the river, bounded by Jalan Raja
Abdullah and Jalan Raja Muda, lies Kampung Baru (translated
as 'New Village'). In this part of the city, things have
not improved much in the past decades and many of the
wooden houses, built in rural kampung style on stilts, have
seen better days.

Which Kampung is Older?

Which kampung is older—Kampung Baru or Kampung
Abdullah Hukum in Bangsar?

Kampung Baru residents are adamant that theirs is
the older kampung and there are some reports using
the adjective 'century-old' to describe it, but evidence
in the form of official records state that it was set up
in 1900.

On the other hand, there is evidence that Kampung
Abdullah Hukum was in existence in the 1890s. The
founder of the kampung, Haji Abdullah Hukum, said in a
1935 newspaper interview that he had obtained
permission from William Maxwell, who became British
Resident in 1889, and Raja Laut to develop the kampung
near what is today called Bangsar.

Kampung Baru is an incongruity in the city, a wooden village lost in a concrete jungle. While spanking new high rise hotels and office blocks costing hundreds of millions of ringgit have sprouted along Jalan Ampang, Kampung Baru moves to its own rhythm.

Famed for its Sunday Market, its pretty mosque and the stalls along Jalan Alang which sell lovely Malay delicacies especially during Ramadhan, the fasting month, Kampung Baru has remained more or less the same since it was set up in 1900 as a Malay Agricultural Settlement. The site was 'practically wasteland covered with coarse grass and bushes and with only a few Chinese squatters on it who did a little gardening and kept pigs'.

The British started the kampung to 'educate the children of the Malays to take part in the administration and to enable them to reap some of the advantages of the present prosperity'.

Today, the government is still trying to get them to reap the advantages of the present prosperity. Efforts to redevelop the area have not been very successful because many lots of land have been inherited by descendants of the original settlers and there are numerous names on the title deeds. Getting all of them to agree on something is no easy task.

The Malay Agricultural Settlement was a move by the British officials to address the problem of the decreasing number of Malay residents in Kuala Lumpur about a hundred years ago.

They allocated 224 acres of land at the outskirts of the Kuala Lumpur in the late 1890s and invited Malays to 'live their natural village life almost within the precincts of a large town'. The Malay settlers were encouraged to plant rice and other crops on their plots of land.

Among the first to settle there were the peons and messengers employed by the government. Later, bullock cart drivers (mostly from Malacca), and foreign Malays like Javanese and Sumatrans moved in. The settlement had practically no native Malays except for the *penghulu* (headman) Raja Mahmud and one or two others. 'Applicants for land generally start by putting up a very small and rough hut, often built of old packing cases and roofed with kerosene oil tins; sometimes this lasts for a couple of years but generally it is replaced by a good-looking and well-built house before the end of that time.' Kampung Baru began in such a humble way.

Ricefields in the Middle of Town

The Malay Agricultural Settlement project, mooted by D.G. Campbell, had another aim—Technical Schools were supposed to be set up to train the Malays in crafts and other skills. Control of the settlement was in the hands of a Board of Management comprising mostly Europeans though the president was the Raja Muda. The Government allocated $6,000 to the settlement annually.

Two silversmiths, one blacksmith, a wood carver, a rattan worker, a tailor, a mat weaver and others were sent to the kampung to take on apprentices and pass on their skills to a younger generation.

They were also supposed to conduct classes at the Malay school in the kampung. It was noble in concept but haphazard in implementation. Reportedly, the scheme 'suffered from a superfluity of ideals insufficiently attached to reality'.

Attempts were made to promote padi planting on swampy land beside the river and some waterwheels were erected for irrigation, but these devices broke into pieces and the experiment in planting padi in the suburbs of an urban area was not quite as successful as the colonials had hoped it would be.

But such was the cycle of life and things went on as usual. In 1924, the responsibility for the maintenance of the settlement was handed over to the Kuala Lumpur Sanitary Board. At that time, there were 544 houses and 2,600 people.

Over the years, the town grew around it and even as more concrete and glass towers were erected, Kampung Baru remained stuck to the old way of doing things.

The disenchantment of the Malays, who felt left out of the economic race and dispossessed in their own land while watching other races, especially the Chinese, accumulating much wealth, reached bursting point and in a flood of fury, the unfortunate 13 May 1969 racial riots erupted. Much of the bloodshed took place in Kampung Baru and neighbouring Chow Kit.

Today, the Government has made one more attempt to transform Kampung Baru, in keeping with its name, into a new settlement, a new neighbourhood.

New Image for the New Village

The first project to kick off the change-the-script agenda for Kampung Baru is Vision City.

Located on 4.5 hectares of land at the junction of Jalan Raja Abdullah and Jalan Sultan Ismail, Vision City will feature three office towers, a four-star business-class hotel, service apartments and a shopping centre.

It is a joint venture between public-listed financial conglomerate Rashid Hussein Berhad and Daewoo Corporation of South Korea.

The estimated cost of Vision City is RM500 million.

It has formed the Konsortium MAS Melayu Berhad, a company comprising Kampung Baru-born businessmen to oversee the redevelopment of the village into a modern settlement of condominiums, apartments, shopping complexes and offices. A hundred lots of land amounting to 96 hectares owned by 2,963 Malays will be involved in the redevelopment.

The Famous Chow Kit

Chow Kit—the man and the place...

Loke Chow Kit is a legendary figure from KL's past. The self-made millionaire was born in Penang to a poor family and his parents scraped enough money to send him to the island's elite educational institution—Penang Free School.

After his education, he made his way south to Kuala Lumpur to seek his fortune. He started off by supplying labourers for the Klang-Kuala Lumpur railway project and since he was a Penangite, his workers were sourced from the island.

After that, he helped to build parts of Klang and with his savings, he invested in tin mines and rubber estates around Kuala Lumpur. Chow Kit also owned a gaming house and opium den at High Street (now called Jalan Tun H.S. Lee) and opened the town's first department store—Chow Kit & Co—which was in the building now occupied by the Industrial Court.

Having made his fortune, he built his first mansion in 1907 at a road now called Jalan Tangsi, within walking distance of the Padang and Selangor Club. This mansion is now occupied by the Malaysian Institute of Architects.

Later, he built another mansion sited in a nine-hectare orchard at Ampang Road which he named Desswood Place, after a road in Aberdeen, Scotland.

A Most Cosmopolitan Man

Chow Kit was a most cosmopolitan man. Educated in English, he socialised well with and was warmly accepted by the colonials. He was also a sporting fellow—a report noted how he shaved his head bald and went to a fancy dress party dressed as a *chetty* (money lender) .

He holidayed overseas regularly and had a special fondness for Scotland, where two of his sons studied in boarding schools.

Since he was so westernised, it was no wonder that his store had a range of goods aimed at the European market. Initially, it was a haberdashery of sorts selling textiles, lace, ribbons and other items. Later, it expanded its range to include liquor, tobacco, cakes and biscuits, foodstuff, glassware and even motorcycles and cars.

His children were often seen in pretty clothes with lace and ribbons from Chow Kit & Co, of course. He lived in style— his household had nine servants including two cooks, a servant to polish his shoes and two gardeners. There was even one worker to run errands for him.

While he was an easygoing chap, he was a businessman to the core—he paid his children 10 cents to massage him before he took a nap daily. And his holidays overseas were also partly to seek new business opportunities. His wealth multiplied many times over, but his empire came to an end when he died in 1918 at the age of 56. His children were too young to take over.

Chow Kit was a well known horse-owner in his time, and was the Steward of the Turf Club. In the Turf Club's centennial celebrations in June 1996, he was honoured with the Loke Chow Kit Stakes.

The Infamous Chow Kit

Jekyll and Hyde of KL ...

Chow Kit is also a place with two faces—the Jekyll and Hyde of KL.

Chow Kit is the section of Kuala Lumpur bounded by Kampung Baru on one side and Jalan Raja Laut on the other, with the main thoroughfare of Jalan Tuanku Abdul Rahman cutting through it. The section starts roughly from the intersection of Jalan Tuanku Abdul Rahman with Jalan Sultan Ismail, to its intersection with Jalan Pahang.

In the daytime, office workers, housewives and shoppers crowd around the place. When the sun sets, and sometimes even before, another set of humanity invades the streets—pleasure seekers and providers. The veneer of respectability is peeled off daily at dusk to reveal Chow Kit's infernal heart that beats with a greater intensity, charging the atmosphere with energy, and making the scene more exciting and exhilarating.

And like a windshield sticker, this veneer of respectability is stuck back on at dawn as the buses and cars ferry the sea of office workers to begin their lives in the safety of their offices.

On the surface, Chow Kit is a bustling community, a warren of shops selling a wide range of goods like drinks, food, clothing, textiles, jewellery, electrical appliances, lottery tickets, household items, cassettes, videos, and shoes. There are also rows of hawkers selling a wide variety of food including one stall which is reputed to sell the best *roti canai* in town and another which has the tastiest *nasi kandar*. Alongside these stalls and shops are respectable .establishments like banks and department stores.

Beneath the surface, or rather behind the facade, it is a totally different story. Many coffeeshops feature a front section with tables and chairs for a quick drink, and a back portion with cubicles for a quicker copulation.

Chicken Rice

While a shop can sell something as innocent as *kai fan* (chicken rice), at the back lane a different kind of *'kai'* (*kai* is Cantonese for 'chicken,' but it is also a slang word for 'prostitute') can be found. A shop at the main road can sell something mundane like shoes or bags, but a few lanes away, a stall will offer the unusual in the form of exotic ointments and feathery gadgets which reputedly can turn a lame duck into a growling tiger in the sexual arena.

From lame duck to growling tiger ...

Chow Kit has possibly the largest number of drug addicts and streetwalkers in the city.

The prostitutes were already hanging out in the area before World War II. Nobody knows why the area became a magnet for the vice merchants, but attract them it did. The Chinatown area of Petaling Street, Sultan Street and High Street had its gambling halls and opium dens, but Chow Kit was where the flesh trade flourished.

A Malay slang term for Chow Kit arose—*belakang mati*. Translated literally as 'dead behind', it came to mean something like a 'dead end' as indeed it was for many people. Society's wretched discards made their way there and lived out their lives with empty looks on their faces with only dreams to drive them on. Ah, if only the next customer would be generous, if only my lottery ticket would strike the first prize....

A few years ago, drug (*'dadah'* in official usage) addicts turned Lorong Haji Taib 6 into the Dadah Alley. There in horrific conditions amidst rotting rubbish, clogged drains and filthy walls, they shot heroin into their bodies wherever they could find a good vein.

Often, they shot into veins in their ankles, thighs and even their more private parts. Sometimes, they got so 'high' that the syringes were still stuck to their bodies when they became semiconscious.

Once, the then Inspector General of Police, *Zombies of* Tan Sri Rahim Noor, visited the backlane and *Chow Kit ...* called them zombies—the living dead of Chow Kit. The 'zombies' were too zonked out to even bother about the top cop's presence.

Cold Turkey

The police moved in and cleared the alley and other backlanes of Chow Kit of drug pushers and addicts. Many of them cold-turkeyed in police lockups. Some were sentenced to jail and some were sent to rehabilitation centres, but when they were released, they returned to Chow Kit.

Official estimates have it that there are some 15,000 addicts in Chow Kit and about 60 cheap hotels which double as brothels. There are also lots of little filthy cubicles where addicts can 'chase the dragon' (breathe in the fumes of heated heroin) or shoot themselves with dirty syringes.

It is said that many of the prostitutes are either addicts or pushers, and numerous cheap hotels and eateries also sell drugs.

Another problem has cropped up recently in the form of illegal Indonesian immigrants who have muscled their way into the small businesses of Chow Kit. It is not unusual to hear conversations in Javanese or some other Indonesian dialect in the Chow Kit stalls.

Every now and then, the authorities move in and clear the place of unlicensed traders and illegal immigrants, but after a spell of lying low, they go back to business.

Renowned Malaysian singer, the late Sudirman, wrote a song about Chow Kit and even performed there in September 1986. The road was closed to traffic and about 100,000 people jammed up the main and side roads to catch a glimpse of the pop star as he paid tribute to the part of the city he had a fondness for.

Urban Renewal

Plans to redevelop the Chow Kit wet market were announced in late 1997 in moves by the authorities to gentrify the area.

Traders in the market at Jalan Raja Bot, which was opened in 1955 by Sultan Hishamuddin Alam Shah, will move to a temporary market at Jalan Ipoh while the redevelopment takes place.

Phase One of the project will feature an 11-storied complex with two floors for the wet market and another for a food court. The upper floors will house retailers, a function hall, a bazaar and four cineplexes. The rooftop will have a public park with jogging track, badminton and squash courts and a swimming pool.

> Construction of Phase One was supposed to take off in 1998 while Phase Two, comprising a 29-storied office tower and an 18-storied three-star hotel, was scheduled to take off in 2000. The total cost involved will be RM800 million.
>
> As soon as the project was announced, however, there were calls to postpone it because of the economic recession, then, due to the turmoil in the currency and stock markets.

Calls to clean up Chow Kit are made every now and then and authorities have announced plans to redevelop the wet market.

Though the process of urban renewal is taking place gradually, Chow Kit will still be haunted by its split personality for many years to come.

A CLOSER LOOK ...

At J. Ampang, you must visit the two little things jutting out of KL's skyline simply because they happen to be the tallest buildings in the world, at least for another year or two. The Petronas Twin Towers are a spectacular sight, the outdoor park is pleasant with great views of skyscrapers, and the fountains are fabulous. The Petronas Towers have also been made into a cultural centre and boasts a world-class concert hall, an art gallery and a museum.

There are malls in the J. Ampang area like the ancient Ampang Park and Plaza Ampang, but these have been upstaged by Suria KLCC, located at the base of the Twin Towers. Suria KLCC is considered by many to be the best designed mall in KL. Although low on heritage hype, its amazing range of products and labels more than make up for that. The musicians, who regularly play on the various floors, add a touch of class while the food court's fare reflects the cosmopolitan nature of today's KL.

At the junction of J. Ampang and J. Sultan Ismail is Concorde Hotel, which houses a joint that is another fave hangout for the local trendies and International School types — Hard Rock Cafe.

The Lake Gardens Area

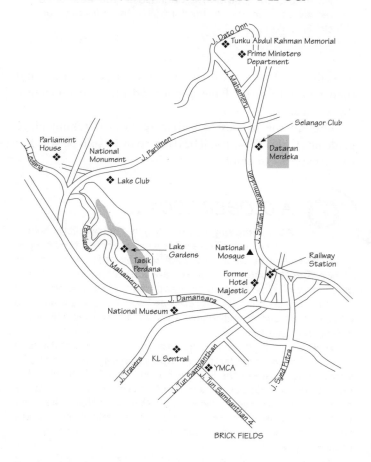

Celebration of Minarets

KL Railway Station
Jalan Sultan Hishamuddin

The romance of the railway journey
has been revived.

KL's railway station—the perfect end to a long journey.

Kuala Lumpur's railway station is the perfect end to a tiring journey. The sight of the fabulous building is bound to revitalise the jaded traveller.

Described as a Byzantine fantasy and a celebration of minarets, it is reputed to be one of the prettiest railway stations in South-east Asia. Indeed the first thing many a tourist would do is head for the railway station to have a look and snap some shots.

Designed by Arthur Benison Hubback, who worked in the Public Works Department and Survey Department of the Federated Malay States, it has remained one of the best architectural legacies from the colonial period.

Designed in 1900, it was completed 11 years later, replacing the wooden structure that served as the town's railway terminal. The original station, built in 1885 near Market Street where the Infokraf building now stands, had merely been an attap shed.

Hubback's station was in two parts—the terminal section comprising offices, waiting rooms and a hotel, and the adjoining train shed.

While the terminal section showed Indian-Muslim and Byzantine influences, the railway shed was definitely English. Hubback borrowed from the glass and iron sheds built in England in that period.

As for the Islamic influence on the arches and minarets, it could have been due to the fact that Hubback had served in the PWD in British India before his posting to Kuala Lumpur. He must have been impressed by the grand Mughal buildings in India.

Though Hubback was tropicalised, so to speak, the building was still influenced by temperate climes—the flat roof of the railway station was built to withstand up to 10 metres of snow.

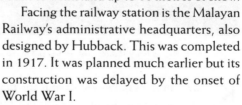

Facing the railway station is the Malayan Railway's administrative headquarters, also designed by Hubback. This was completed in 1917. It was planned much earlier but its construction was delayed by the onset of World War I.

A Room with a View

There is a great aura of romance about travelling by train; and some hope that this aura extends itself to the station as well.

After being left vacant for many years, the Station Hotel (which occupies one wing of the Kuala Lumpur Railway Station) was reopened by Taiwanese investor and architect, Mr Lim Chung Ming in January 1996. Renamed the Heritage Station Hotel of Kuala Lumpur, it has 176 rooms and suites, a restaurant, a health centre, a ballroom which can accommodate 800 people, a conference and a rooftop swimming pool.

Mr Lim is no stranger to operating railway station hotels—he runs the station hotels in Tanjong Pagar in Singapore, Johor Baru and the Majestic Station Hotel in Ipoh. He dreams of running a chain of station hotels from Singapore to China. Now, that is one hotelier with the heart of a true traveller.

To indicate that the two buildings were designed as a pair, Hubback used a smaller version of the railway station's minaret to crown the main dome of the administrative building.

These two beautiful buildings have contributed much to the identity of Kuala Lumpur as an oriental city and capital of an Islamic nation.

It is said that Hubback put all his energy, heart, and soul into the railway station and railway administrative headquarters as he died soon after their completion.

One wing of the railway station was rebuilt rather clumsily in recent times, and when major refurbishments were embarked on in 1986, the earlier renovation was re-renovated and made harmonious with the design and character of the building.

Colonial Style with a
Dash of YMCA

Jalan Sultan Hishamuddin

Will Hotel Majestic ever stage its
magnificent comeback?

When the Kuala Lumpur Hilton was taking shape in 1970, one writer noted that the Hotel Majestic was 'as out-of-date as a pith helmet'.

But the Hotel Majestic was already out of date for a long time before that; its days of majesty were in the 1930s, lasting till the Federal Hotel in Bukit Bintang opened in 1957.

And being out of date was its main attraction. Its very quaintness attracted the true travellers who were looking for romantic sojourns. Dining beneath a huge dome with the large doors providing a fabulous view of the small garden, the minarets of the railway station across the road and a flock of swallows swirling in mid-air was quite an experience.

Hotel Majestic, designed by Dutch architect Van Leangeanderg, was built in 1932 on the site of a bungalow and garden formerly occupied by the German Consul during World War I. It had 51 large airy rooms with spacious toilets and oval long baths with metal legs shaped like lion's paws. In the rooms were heavy beds, closets, hatstands, chairs and side tables made of teak. The chandelier-like lights could be dimmed by lowering them with a pulley system.

The furnishing was described as functional—'colonial-style with a dash of YMCA'.

One report said 'the rooms are vast—personal warehouses designed for the P & O pre-jet days when luggage was almost exclusively huge trunks'.

In its halcyon period, it was the toast of the town—its rooftop nightclub was the venue of countless parties, weddings and consulate receptions.

Hotel Majestic was touted to be Kuala Lumpur's Raffles Hotel. Planters from out of town had the choice of staying there or across the road at Station hotel at the railway station. The financially-challenged went to the Coliseum. White travellers and businessmen stayed at the Majestic. A writer said the Majestic was 'one of those Somerset Maugham-type places—it was in those days when the white topi and feathered hat are hung on hooks after a cricket game'.

Another poetically described it as 'a museum of colonial murmurs'. During World War II, a different set of colonialists checked in—the Japanese invaders who used it as a transit camp. When the war ended, one officer took the news of his country's surrender so badly that he committed suicide and it has been rumoured that his room— **Suicide in** No. 48—was haunted by his troubled spirit. **room 48 ...**

Character's Club

In its years of operation, it has seen all sorts of troubled or free spirits. So much so that one writer said it 'is more than a hotel— it is a character's club'.

There was an Irish woman who locked herself in her room for 10 days surviving only on orange juice for the purpose of finishing her novel. There was an Englishman who claimed that he was in town to conduct a census on the dragonfly population using a special ultrasonic device. An old white man was overheard claiming that he was the illegitimate son of Sherlock Holmes.

Artists, writers, actors (such as David Niven), travellers and romantics have stayed at Hotel Majestic. And politicians too. In the old days, the founders of the United Malay National Organisation (UMNO), which is now the prominent member of the National Front coalition government, stayed at the hotel and held meetings there, plotting to win independence from the British. Dato Onn Jaafar and Tunku Abdul Rahman were frequent guests. Dato Onn Jaafar passed on the leadership of UMNO to Tunku during a meeting at the rooftop of the Majestic. Even the Malayan Chinese Association (MCA), the Chinese-based political party, held their formative meetings there.

Spies turned up at the Majestic during the war, making contact with their informers at the bar. That was replaced in 1954 with an 'attractive cocktail bar, the only one of its kind in Malaya' designed and constructed under the personal supervision of Lim Jit Hee, the managing director of the hotel.

The sides were cushioned in red Vinatex with the top of the counter covered in mistletoe-green onyx Formica which was also used for the showcase, part of the wall and window.

Under the counter was a 'modern Kelvinator Beer Cooler'. The whole lounge 'presents a most pleasing appearance of good taste and is one that will become popular with patrons of the Hotel Majestic'.

But the patrons of the hotel did not go there just for drinks at the bar. They went for lunch and tea and they would fondly remember the white linen, starched so stiff that the folds could almost cut, the silver teapots and porcelain cups and saucers stamped with the hotel's logo. Of course, how could anybody forget the waiters? They were Chinamen, as old as the hotel and as slow as a steam-powered train, but they mumbled politely and did not mix up the orders.

Some guests even turned the hotel into their home—Mrs Buxton, High Commissioner Sir Gerald Templer's secretary; Donald Davies, who was well known in Kuala Lumpur's thespian circles; and Mrs Dorothy Nixon of the Selangor Book Club. The latter two lived in the hotel for more than 20 years and died there.

Behind the hotel lived a troop of monkeys and many guests have been scared out of their wits by them. A story goes that a female guest

Monkeying around ...

ran naked into the corridor screaming when a hairy intruder made its way into her room while she was taking a bath.

In 1976, there was a proposal to demolish the hotel to build a 22-storeyed office building at its site. Along the way, the plan was shelved and Hotel Majestic survived for another seven years.

The era of Hotel Majestic finally ended on 31 December 1983.

After renovations, it reopened as the National Art Gallery in the middle of 1984. As an indication of the low priority given the arts, the National Art Gallery had been squatting at Tunku Abdul Rahman Hall at Jalan Ampang since 1959 (which has since reopened as MATIC, the Malaysian Tourist Information Centre). There were calls to retain Hotel Majestic as a hotel and shift the gallery to Central Market instead, but the authorities did not budge.

Finally, A Home for Art

The RM45-million new National Art Gallery at Jalan Tun Razak is the first building in Malaysia built purposely for art exhibitions. It has a theatrette, a creative centre, an art library and archives, exhibition space, photographic studio and surau (prayer room).

Its first floor boasts a cafe, gallery shop, VIP lounge, sculpture gallery and temporary exhibition hall. On the second floor is the hall for the permanent exhibition of some 2,000 works while the third floor has space for photographic displays.

When the building was completed in November 1998, the National Art Gallery finally had a permanent address.

Last Waltz

On 16 December 1983, a last ball was held at Hotel Majestic. It was a masquerade theme party and the restaurant was decorated in pink and blue and the cream of Kuala Lumpur society turned up in tuxedos and BMWs.

On 31 December, nine guests checked in just to experience the passing of a memorable hotel. No New Year's Eve gala dinner party was held and the mood at Hotel Majestic was one of gloom. While other hotels were filled with revellers having fun and ushering in the new year with crackers and tooters, Hotel Majestic was filled with poignancy as the guests basked in memories.

During the night, someone broke into a storeroom and made off with 10 silver teapots and some porcelain ones. It was probably the work of a souvenir hunter. Other souvenir hunters turned up a few days later for an auction of all the fittings.

The furniture sets—plus bath tubs—were sold on a room by room basis and they fetched between $350 and $900. The most popular items were the sets of six tea cups and saucers and milk jug which fetched up to $250 per set. Somebody paid $200 for the English phone booth.

$200 for an English phone booth...

While the auction was proceeding, someone made off with six green wooden benches. Apparently, the person had paid a hotel staff $60 before loading the benches on a lorry and driving off.

One person bought the fittings of the room he spent his honeymoon in, only to discover that the furniture had been changed. Another found the items that he bought at the auction missing when he returned later with a lorry to take them away.

In that sad fashion, Hotel Majestic was dissected, dismembered and disembowelled.

Recently, Hotel Majestic was supposed to be restored to its former glory and given a new lease of life. Public-listed company Yeoh Tiong Lay (YTL) Corporation Berhad, which built the new National Art Gallery, was given a 90-year lease on the former Hotel Majestic building.

It was originally going to be re-converted into a hotel. According to the earlier plans, the new Hotel Majestic was to be a classic period hotel featuring old-world splendour which would have fit in well with the concept of the Eastern and Oriental Express train service that YTL operates on the Singapore-Bangkok route. YTL was amassing a collection of old Hotel Majestic memorabilia for exhibition at the new hotel which was supposed to open in time to usher in the year 2000.

However, due to the recession of 1997/98 and the drastic drop in tourism, that plan has been put on hold and the current proposal is to turn the former hotel into a university campus.

The 15th Mile

Jalan Tun Sambanthan

Though the brickkilns have closed,
Brickfields has kept its name.

Some old Chinese folks still call it 'The 15th Mile' ('Sap Ng Pei' in Cantonese) while most other KLites know it as Brickfields, even though the only bricks you find these days are on the walls of buildings.

Brickfields got its name from the many brickkilns located there during the building boom in the 1880s. In 1886, as buildings mushroomed all over town, there were 15 brickkilns and six limekilns in Kuala Lumpur, and these were mostly sited in the area now known as Brickfields.

Yap Ah Loy was one of the major players in the brick industry then. So was Resident Frank Swettenham, who owned a 'brick-making company' using his wife as a front man. It was Swettenham's replanning and rebuilding of Kuala Lumpur which created the sudden increase in demand for bricks in the first place. Today's financial watchdogs would call that insider trading.

Brickfields got its Chinese name because it was 15 miles from Damansara along the old track to Kuala Lumpur. Travellers sailed upriver from Klang, disembarked at Damansara and rode ponies or bullock carts along a rough track to Kuala Lumpur.

Brickfields today has other landmarks, such as the YMCA, where backpackers on budget holidays head to, and The Pines, a row of eateries serving Chinese and seafood dishes.

Brickfields also housed many Malayan Railways staff, and some of their old quarters are still standing.

The small area has a surprisingly large number of religious landmarks such as Kuala Lumpur's only Neo-Gothic church, located along the main road.

The Church of the Holy Rosary was built in 1903 under the supervision of Reverend J.F. Lambert, a French missionary. But the congregation of worshippers there had been established much earlier, in 1883, to serve the needs of the Chinese community in the town.

Other religious landmarks include the Zion Evangelical Lutheran Church built in 1924, the Vivekananda Ashram built in 1904 and the Buddhist Maha Vihaya built in 1894. Every year when Vesak Day is celebrated, thousands of Buddhists follow a procession which starts from the Buddhist temple.

Another landmark, which is spiritual in form if not substance, is the only licensed toddy stall in Kuala Lumpur at Jalan Berhala. Toddy, a wine made from the fermented sap of a type of palm tree, is sweet if well-made and always potent. It is a drink associated with the poor and with Malaysians having become richer and **Potent wine ...** acquiring a taste for ice beers in pubs, the toddy stall has experienced diminishing business.

Some years ago, Brickfields had some red-light entertainment areas, but these have been gentrified in recent times when several upmarket condominiums were built there.

Brickfields also had a cinema (now demolished) called Lido, (known as Prince's Cinema in the prewar days), which screened Kuala Lumpur's first talking movie.

The face of Brickfields will change forever when the billion-ringgit KL Sentral project is completed on land belonging to Malayan Railways.

Central City

Many building projects stalled in 1997, when the regional recession occurred as a result of the collapse of the Thai baht. Kuala Lumpur, the capital city, is where most of these massive constructions are sited and even today, half-built projects can be seen all over the city.

On a large tract of land at Brickfields—open and pleasant to most KL residents, but underutilised and in dire need of reinvestment to town planners and businessmen—that used to be occupied by warehouses, railway yards and dilapidated railway staff quarters, a new transportation terminal is being built.

Called Kuala Lumpur Sentral, the city-within-a-city project is on 29 hectares of land and the final phase is scheduled for completion by the year 2007 though it may take longer now. The entire project is estimated to cost RM3 billion.

Bounded by Jalan Travers and Jalan Tun Sambanthan, the project will turn the hitherto sleepy Brickfields into the transportation hub of Kuala Lumpur.

KL Sentral is touted to become a vital centre for business and commerce. It will have the only direct rail link to the new Kuala Lumpur International Airport at Sepang via the Express Rail Link (ERL). Work on the ERL was stalled for a while and the government recently pushed for the completion of this project, which will also ensure the success of the other megaproject, the new Kuala Lumpur International Airport (KLIA) in Sepang.

KL Sentral, which is developed by public-listed Malaysian Resources Corporation Berhad, will also be the City Air Terminal where passengers can check-in their luggage, confirm their flights and travel 35 minutes on the fast train to the KLIA.

The new Stesyen Sentral Kuala Lumpur will become the main platform of interchange for the city's new Light Rail Transport (LRT), Express Rail Link, the electric KTM Komuter train service and the existing North-South railway line that goes to Singapore and Thailand.

The station will have 12 platforms, 28 tracks and five concourse areas which are designed to handle up to 99 million travellers per year by 2020. The existing railway station services about 5.4 million people per annum.

Travellers entering Malaysia through KL Sentral will be able to book hotel rooms, hire cars, confirm flights and change money at the one-stop centre where air, rail and road communications meet. It will be an intelligent set-up with computerised linkages via fibre optics and satellite.

The Stesyen Sentral Kuala Lumpur was supposed to have been completed in 1998 to synchronise with the completion of the new airport in Sepang. Work on it stopped when the financial crisis hit Malaysia and it has just resumed.

Other than the station, the first phase of KL Sentral will include the 52-storeyed MRCB Tower, corporate suites, condominiums, retail outlets, service apartments, hotels and office buildings.

It will also have an auditorium, a sports and recreation centre, more than 30 acres of landscaped gardens and 16,000 parking bays.

Venning's Labour of Love for Lovers

Jalan Parlimen

Botanic Gardens attracts more lovers than horticulturists.

The Lake Gardens in Kuala Lumpur, now called Taman Tasik Perdana, has always been the place to be—not so much for nature lovers as courting couples.

To tease a couple that they look tired because they had spent the previous night at Lake Gardens means that they had been out courting and romancing. The numerous shady trees and cosy corners have always been alcoves for lovers.

To discourage such activities, the authorities often throw a spanner in the works for many couples and after the disruption, the lovers are reprimanded. These days, sodium street lamps have been erected all over the park to dampen the enthusiasm of lovers.

A few years ago, there was a newspaper report about City Hall responding to a complaint that its officers doubled as peeping toms. City Hall replied: 'The officers were placed there to ensure the safety of the people and prevent unwanted incidents. If couples and lovebirds saw them while they were having a good time, it was only pure coincidence.'

The lovers—and the few nature lovers—have to thank Alfred Venning, the chairman of the Sanitary Board and State Treasurer of Selangor, for this beautiful park that Kuala Lumpur boasts. But Venning had intended it to be a botanic garden rather than a lovers' haunt.

In 1888, he proposed to Swettenham that a botanic garden should be laid out in the long ravine on the outskirts of the town—'several acres of swamp, in which briars and lallang, forest trees, screw pines and tree ferns were interspersed in picturesque confusion'.

Swettenham and Venning spent several mornings scouting the forested area and finally, Swettenham agreed to the concept and approved the allocation of some Government money.

Over the next 10 years, Venning gradually cleared the forest and laid out a park of 173 acres. Though enlarged, today's Lake Gardens is not very different from what Venning had created. He had some experience in horticulture as he had been a planter in Ceylon.

Scrub and lallang were cut, wild plants and common trees were uprooted and replanted with ornamental and flowering trees and shrubs, and 'an experimental economic garden' was laid out. Venning attracted the support of many people in KL in what they recognised as his labour of love.

Towkay Ah Yeok contributed a hundred white chempaka and orange trees. A construction engineer called Gordon dammed up the Bras Bras River to create a lake which was named Sydney lake, after Constance Sydney Holmes, Swettenham's wife.

Raja Brookes and Astronomy

The Lake Gardens area is one of the most popular tourist destinations in Kuala Lumpur—in fact, it was expanded for that purpose.

Initially, the Orchid Park was set up—a place where colourful and exotic orchids were grown and enthusiasts could gather every weekend to exchange information and pick up some new varieties.

Behind it lay the Hibiscus Park. Since the hibiscus, or *bunga raya* in Malay, is Malaysia's national flower, the park was seen as more significant even though the orchids are just as pretty.

All sorts of hybrids can be seen at the Hibiscus Park and there is even one named after the Prime Minister.

Nearby, the Deer Park lets visitors feed the tame animals. Look closely in the undergrowth and the tiny *kancil*, the small and shy mousedeer, can be seen.

Opposite the Orchid Park is the Bird Park. Over the years, some birds have started breeding inside the park and many have become used to the presence of humans, such as the hornbills, which love to pick up scraps of food from those eating at the balcony of the fast-food outlet near the park's entrance.

Down the road is the Butterfly Park where winged beauties flutter all around visitors and land on flowers to feast on nectar.

A bungalow which used to be the residence of the second Prime Minister, Tun Razak, has been converted into a memorial complete with his collection of walking sticks, his extensive library and his favourite reading chair.

Nearby is the National Planetarium, housing exhibits on astronomy, a telescope and a special theatre with a hemispheric screen. Replicas of ancient Indian and Chinese observatories and England's mysterious Stonehenge are found near the entrance of the planetarium.

The planetarium is now connected by a pedestrian bridge to the Muzium Negara (National Museum) which was recently refurbished with a new administration block.

Fine Sheet of Water

Lake Gardens was formally opened on 13 May 1889 by the Governor of the Straits Settlements, Sir Cecil Clementi Smith, who was on a visit to Kuala Lumpur. It rained heavily on that day, but it did not spoil the event and before a large gathering of KL's colonial elite, he officially named the 'fine sheet of water' and declared the gardens open.

Very quickly, the Lake Gardens was the place to go to for relaxing strolls amidst pretty greenery and flowering plants. There was music too—there were afternoon concerts by the

Police Band. The band regularly played at the Padang but on Thursdays, it performed at Lake Gardens.

These days, there are occasional musical performances at the Panggung Anniversary, an outdoor stadium near the Lake Club. People still go to the Lake Gardens for the quietude or to jog. And to court, of course.

In 1937, it was a common pastime for Europeans and some adventurous locals to explore the ravines to the north and west of the Lake Gardens. One could enter a ravine at Maxwell Road (now Jalan Tun Ismail) and follow the trail to emerge at Damansara Road near the entrance to Lake Gardens. Some even rode horses in the ravines.

The same year, the British Resident, S.W. Jones, reported: 'Quite a number of common lowland birds may be seen in the Lake Gardens. Black Panther, Golden Cats (Rimau Daun), Honey Bears and a small pack of wild dogs have been seen in these ravines following in the trail of their food supply which consists of monkeys, mouse deer and small ground animals.'

Back then, Lake Gardens was pretty wild territory, quite like an open menagerie. Now it is encircled by highways. The ravines have been filled up and the only animals to be found are stuffed ones in the nearby Muzium Negara (National Museum) and some tame ones at the Deer Park.

Birds still abound, but most live in captivity at the Bird Park.

Monument with a Chequered Past

The National Monument

Jalan Parlimen

A bomb explosion shatters a country's monument, but not its pride...

If anyone finds some resemblance, in style or theme, between the National Monument in Kuala Lumpur and the famed Iwo Jima monument in Washington, United States of America, he or she should not be accused of being overimaginative. The same sculptor did both works.

Tunku Abdul Rahman, the first Prime Minister, visited Washington in 1960 and was awestruck by the Iwo Jima monument.

Awestruck by Iwo Jima ...

It moved him so much that he decided to commission the sculptor, Felix de Weldon, to design one for his own country to commemorate those who died during the Emergency (1948–1960).

On 31 July 1961, Tunku launched the National Monument Fund and in an outpouring of patriotism, all sorts of events such as talentimes and dance shows were organised to raise funds. In many towns, there were Monument Queen beauty pageants. In Kuala Lumpur, contests were held to pick a Miss Pretty Feet and a Miss Stylish Hair.

Radio Malaya charged a fee for each song request, while the football authorities donated 2% of the ticket sales of the 1961 Malaya Cup final.

The 44 staff of the Selangor Information Office contributed 4% of their salary, while the government put in $200,000.

The first donor to the Fund was (later Tun) Ismail Mohamed Ali, Deputy Governor of Bank Negara (Malaysia's Central Bank). Bank Negara was also the treasurer of the Fund. He donated $50 inclusive of a $25 fine for speaking English to the Tunku during the National Language Month.

There were donors from outside the country—some foreigners and some Malayans working overseas.

A message of support was received from Major General Bela Kiraly, commander-in-chief of the Hungarian Freedom Fighters during the Budapest Revolt of 1956. He could identify with the anti-communist theme of the National Monument. The group, which existed in exile in New York, donated $713.

A three-man team of East German refugees who visited Malaya donated 200 marks.

Raising Funds

Three Malayans working in a phosphate mine on Christmas Island donated $365, possibly a dollar for each day of the year. Five Malayan pearl divers from Broome, Western Australia, sent 12 Australian pounds and 10 shillings (about $80 then).

Even the American expatriate community in Kuala Lumpur got into the act and organised an All-Asia premier of *My Geisha* starring Shirley Maclaine and Yves Montand at Cathay cinema on 16 March 1962, and raised $12,118.

Teen idol and pop star Cliff Richard, who held a concert in Kuala Lumpur in 1962, contributed $1,000.

The donations simply rolled in, and money was not a problem.

There were no hitches until the monument was unveiled. Many criticised the monument, saying that the soldiers looked too Caucasian. One critic even **Not local** pointed out that their hats resembled those worn **enough ...** by Australian and New Zealander soldiers during the Emergency. An ex-British serviceman wrote to say that only the two fallen soldiers, representing dead communists, had local features.

Typically Malaysian

'The features are reduced to their classical proportions. It is a composite cross section of the Malaysian soldier. The figures have high cheekbones which are typically Malaysian. They have no European features. Everything is idealised for the purpose of beauty,' said the sculptor, Felix de Weldon, who was rebutting criticism that the monument was too Caucasian and did not reflect a Malaysian identity.

There were some grounds for rebuttal. The uniforms were Malayan because a sample had been sent to Felix de Weldon and when he was working in his Washington studio, a member of the Malayan Embassy staff had been his model.

Furthermore, the central figure of the National Monument, an unarmed soldier holding the flag, was supposed to resemble Tunku in his younger days.

The monument was created in Washington in plaster and cast in the Via Appia foundry in Rome, Italy. The 6-metre tall figures arrived at Port Swettenham (now called Port Klang) by ship in June 1965.

Felix flew in and selected the spot to erect the monument with Tunku. It was on a hill overlooking the Lake Gardens and the newly-built Parliament House. To make way for the National Monument, a Malay palace, Istana Hinggap, was demolished. It had been the Kuala Lumpur residence of the Yang di-Pertuan Besar of Negri Sembilan, and had been his property since 1951.

Thus the symbol of peace and freedom and a nation's determination to forge ahead against all odds, even communist terrorists, came into being. The fallen figures symbolise the enemy and evil. The two with Bren guns symbolise victory and patriotism. The wounded and another helping him symbolise sacrifice and brotherly love while the unarmed soldier holding the flag, and modelled after Tunku, represents spiritual and leadership values. The dedication on the base is in English and Jawi—'Dedicated to the heroic fighters in the cause of peace and freedom. May the blessing of Allah be upon them.'

Templer's View

Tun Sir Gerald Templer, British High Commissioner and Director of Operations during the Emergency years of 1951–54, visited the monument with his wife in April 1966. His verdict? 'One of the finest in the world, and I have seen a lot of monuments.'

The Peace is Shattered

The $1.5 million monument to commemorate the 11,073 people who died during the Emergency was opened by the Yang di-Pertuan Agong on 8 February 1966, and among the guests were visiting Korean president Park Chung Hee and his wife. Felix presented Tunku with 44 Long Play records of Koran reading and a luminous manuscript of the Koran.

Thousands of Malaysians headed for the latest attraction in town. Tourists dropped by on city tours and took lots of snapshots. Postcards featuring the National Monument went on sale. Commemorative stamps were issued.

After a while, the National Monument became something that was always there, like an old building or landmark, and the nation went about its normal business. Tourists still turned up by the bus loads and clicked away. All was quiet and peaceful at the national monument except for some overenthusiastic courting couples who happened to linger at the more remote corners of the monument complex.

Then the peace was shattered when a *A bomb* bomb exploded prematurely just before dawn *explosion ...* on 26 August 1975.

The communists, who had resurrected their campaign to destabilise the government and turned their struggle into urban terrorism, had chosen to destroy the very symbol of their defeat to demoralise the populace.

At least four terrorists, believed to be from the Malayan National Liberation Front section of the Malayan Communist Party, including one woman, had planted time bombs all over the monument designed to blast it into smithereens. One bomb went off accidentally, injuring at least one of the terrorists who left a trail of blood. In their hurry to escape on scooters, the communists left two crash helmets and an identity card.

Among the first to be at the scene was (by then, ex-Prime Minister) Tunku Abdul Rahman, who was performing his morning prayers when he heard the explosion at 5 am. He rushed there with a cine camera but in his haste, he forgot to load the film.

The National Monument today—symbol of a country's pride.

What he saw must have shocked him—one figure holding a Bren gun was on the floor in pieces while the two figures representing dead communists were 'beheaded'. Perhaps as a sign of providence, the central figure, the young Tunku lookalike, was relatively undamaged.

Two time bombs were still ticking away and they were defused by the bomb squad later. They were timed to explode when the morning guard parade took place.

The Malaysian people were shocked by the bold act, but their resolve was not broken and they were still as generous as ever.

Raising Funds Again

Prime Minister Tun Razak set up a restoration fund within weeks and there was another round of fund-raising activities. In a replay of events that took place in the early sixties, there were all sorts of concerts, parties and functions to raise funds to repair national pride.

Reassembling the Cenotaph

The National Monument complex includes several fountains, a semicircle of pavilions and a Cenotaph near the entrance.

The Cenotaph was originally placed at Victory Avenue (now called Jalan Sultan Hishamuddin) near the railway station. The granite Cenotaph was built in 1921 to commemorate the fallen Commonwealth troops in World War I. Later, names of those who fell in World War II and the Emergency were added to the roll of honour.

It was taken apart piece by piece in November 1961 and reassembled at its present site when the National Monument was built.

Popular singer Saloma performed. There were donations from Filipino and Gurkha soldiers. And 10 communist detainees gave $180.

A film premiere of *Seniman Silam* at Kuala Lumpur's Federal cinema raised $91,601. *The Odessa File* premiered in a new cinema in Sitiawan and raised $22,241.

A lecturer with the Institut Teknologi Mara School of Art and Design, Christopher Carny, was commissioned to restore the monument and he resorted to using new methods for the job.

With help from Terengganu craftsmen and students from ITM—Mufti Jantan, Zulkifli Maulana and Hamid Hassan—the monument was repaired in a year at a cost of $200,000. There were some attempts to 'Malaysianise' the faces of the damaged figures, but it was never officially disclosed how successful these attempts were. Three gold mosaic domes were also repaired and a decorative-cum-security fence built at a cost of $400,000. The restoration fund had raised $1,325,092 and the remainder went to the Heroes' Welfare Fund.

By mid-1977, the National Monument was reopened and the tourists and curious locals returned by the thousands.

Courting couples, however, had to find other remote corners for their nocturnal trysts—the National Monument was locked up after dusk.

Desirable Dwelling

Persiaran Mahameru

Malaysia's very own Raffles Hotel?

Perched on a hilltop overlooking a pretty garden below the balcony, with verdant scenery just beyond its fence and the blue hills of the Main Range in the distance, Carcosa is everybody's dream home. Currently, it is perhaps the only hotel in Malaysia which can match the Raffles in Singapore in terms of grandeur and history.

Carcosa, that colonial gem, was the house that Frank Swettenham built—and lived in.

Swettenham had an illustrious career as the Resident General of the Federated Malay States and Governor of Singapore. Being the Englishman that he was, with the very English aspiration of living in a country estate, he built a home befitting his station in life.

The origin of that exotic non-English non-Malay name — Carcosa remained a mystery for a good many years till somebody contacted the builder himself in 1936 for clarification. Swettenham had by then been living in retirement in the West End of London.

Built in 1898 at a cost of $67,000, the mansion was named Carcosa by Swettenham, who came across it in the dedicatory verses at the front of a book of horror stories called *The King In Yellow* by Robert Chambers which had the following:

Along the shore the cloud waves break,
The twin suns sink beneath the lake,
The shadows lengthen in Carcosa.

Strange is the night where black stars rise,
And twin moons circle through the skies,
But stranger still is Lost Carcosa.

Songs that the Hyades shall sing,
Where flap the tatters of the king,
Must die unheard in Dim Carcosa.

Song of my soul, my voice is dead,
Die thou unsung as tears unshed
Shall dry and die in Lost Carcosa

Cassilda's song in *The King In Yellow*, Act I Scene 2.

Swettenham opined that the name had been 'created by the author's fancy though it looks like a combination of the Italian words *cara* and *casa* and would mean "desirable dwelling" as indeed, I found it.'

Swettenham himself had been very much involved in the building of his desirable dwelling. In 1896, he picked a choice piece of land on a hill overlooking the Lake Gardens and in the distance, the hills of the interior. In his time, there was still much greenery around and often, deer strayed into the park below. And birds would land on branches near his balcony and break into song.

It is not known if Swettenham was ever introduced to the Chinese geomantic art of *feng shui*, but the site he chose was indeed favourable.

Good fengshui ...

Palace-Warming Bash

The newspapers called it 'Mr Swettenham's Palace' and indeed it was as imposing as a palace. Though someone commented that it 'stood out uncomfortably on the skyline,' Carcosa was still the grandest mansion in Kuala Lumpur at that time.

According to H.S. Barlow, a fancy dress ball was held on 29 August 1898 to celebrate the opening of Carcosa and the theme was based on *Unaddressed Letters*, a book by Swettenham which was published earlier that year featuring a picture of Swettenham wearing a hat looking rather 'dapper' framed by the doorway of a wooden house.

The next day, *The Malay Mail* reported: 'Carcosa of course lends itself admirably to the entertainment of a large number of guests, but it would indeed have to be a brilliant assembly to surpass the effect produced upon the mind by the gaily dressed and laughing throng which crowded the beautiful rooms and verandahs of the Resident-General's palatial house last night.'

The newspaper carried a list of attendees and it was like a Who's Who of the colonial community. There were only three natives—the Kapitan Cina, Thamboosamy Pillai and Loke Yew.

'Mrs Baxendale, wife of the head of the Public Works Department appeared as Unaddressed Letters, in a yellow dress, embroidered with white fleurs-de-lys, in imitation of the cover of the book,' wrote Barlow.

'The genial Dr Travers was dressed as Ally Sloper, the hero of a London weekly magazine, *Ally Sloper's Half Holiday*, which humorously chronicled Ally Sloper's escapades attempting to ascend the upper reaches of high society.'

The musicians comprising the Perak and Selangor bands struck up in harmony, the spirits flowed freely and the revellers danced till their feet ached and a few tipsy guests must have made their way to a remoter corner for a snooze because the party lasted till dawn.

Swettenham had a special fondness for Carcosa and he actually used the name Carcosa as the telegraphic code for Resident-General.

A beautiful house on the hill—is Carcosa KL's answer to Singapore's Raffles Hotel?

A.C. Norman has been credited with designing the building though Spooner claimed that he was the 'guiding hand' behind its design. Regardless of who the designer was, there was undoubtedly enthusiastic input from Swettenham, probably because he had been instrumental in designing and building the house for the British Resident, The Residency, on another hilltop overlooking the Gombak River, and he never got to stay in it. This time, he planned a grander mansion and made sure that he stayed there.

But when Swettenham returned to this part of the world as Resident-General of the FMS in June 1896, he was temporarily given the use of the Government Secretary's house in Lake Gardens, near where today's War Memorial and National Monument are. This was later known as the Old Carcosa and one wonders if this could be the Istana Hinggap which was demolished to make way for the National Monument in the early 1960s.

Classy Abode

Swettenham's biographer, Barlow, says: 'Initially conditions were rough. The whole place was drenched every time it rained. But ultimately he was not to live in discomfort: $8,000 was sanctioned for furniture. Nevertheless it was cramped and unsuitable for entertaining: when Swettenham gave a dance there on 5 November 1896, supper had to be served in two shifts.'

By the end of June 1896, the site for the new house for the Resident-General had already been chosen, to the west of the Lake Gardens.

Swettenham was said to have been very satisfied with the chocolate and cream tiles that covered the ground floor verandah and his private rooms which were 'surrounded by a verandah laid with Minton Hollins ornamental floor tiles imported from Switzerland'.

Countless tea and dinner parties were held on the lush grounds of the mansion, not to mention formal receptions and indoor dinners, candlelit undoubtedly, peppered with polite small talk, waltzing and tittering. What gossip, what news, what secrets—state or personal—the walls must have overheard...

Swettenham stayed there till he became the Governor of Singapore in 1901, upon which he moved to the Government House in Singapore.

Carcosa has always served as the home of top British officials, such as the Resident-General, Chief Secretary, Federal Secretary and British Resident of Selangor.

During World War II, a Japanese general moved in and later, it became an officers' mess. After the war, it continued as an officers' mess—for the British soldiers this time. Later, it resumed its role as the home of the Chief Secretary.

Its last occupant was Sir David Watherson, who acted as host to the Duke of Gloucester when he came as representative of the Queen to present the constitutional instruments to Tunku Abdul Rahman in recognition of Malaya's independence in 1957.

The Tunku graciously presented Carcosa to the British Government to be used as the High Commissioner's home. This state of affairs continued till almost 30 years later, when rising nationalistic emotions forced the Malaysian Government to claim it back from the British on 1 August 1986.

A short walk from Carcosa is the Istana Tetamu, another grand building which was called King's House in colonial times. This was built in 1904 by the Federal Malay States Government as the residence of the Governor of the Straits Settlements. Istana Tetamu was used as a Government guest house for VIPs and those who have stayed in it included the Shah of Iran, Queen Elizabeth II, the Emperor of Ethiopia, President Johnson and President Marcos.

Carcosa and Istana Tetamu, later renamed Seri Negara, were refurbished into classical hotels offering 13 luxurious suites. Carcosa Seri Negara opened on 1 November 1989 featuring a kind of ostentation that was rare in Kuala Lumpur. There were thick carpets, gold-plated faucets, jacuzzis, silver forks and spoons, fine bone chinaware, crystal chandeliers and four-poster beds. The restaurant served nouveau cuisine, fine wines, and cigars and cognac with coffee.

Queen Elizabeth stayed there a few years ago and the suite she was in, the Seri Ehsan suite, has been renamed Queen's Suite. Prince Philip stayed just next door and that suite is now called Duke's Suite.

After all these years, Carcosa still resonates with the presence of the British.

The Resident's Residence

Jalan Dato Onn

The Residency has the distinction of having been the home of the first British Resident, the first Chief Minister and the first Prime Minister of Malaysia.

The Residency

The Residency is the other house that Frank Swettenham built which he never got to live in.

Tracing the history of the Residency will lead the historian to Klang where Captain Bloomfield Douglas, who became British Resident in 1876, was rather wary of being under attack and his Residency in that town 'had all the appearance of an armed post amidst a hostile population'.

When the State capital moved from Klang to Kuala Lumpur, he selected a hill overlooking the Gombak river as the site for his new Residency. There, he planned to construct a 'redoubt' from which he could fire at will at Kuala Lumpur's town centre if necessary. But his superiors (Sir Frederick Weld, who was then Administrator based in Singapore, and Swettenham, who was the Assistant Colonial Secretary at that time) decided against his plans as they were not so afflicted by the siege mentality. And the State Government was a bit low on funds anyway. Thus it was decided to dismantle the Residency and other government buildings in Klang and ship them upriver to Kuala Lumpur for reassembly.

Nevertheless, Douglas turned the Residency into a makeshift fort by installing a howitzer at its terrace and 'enlivened gubernatorial visits by target practice in the direction of the jungle outskirts'.

That Residency in Klang was a spacious double-storeyed timber building constructed by Tunku Kudin for the first British Resident in Selangor, J.G. Davidson, who arrived in December 1874. When Davidson was sent to Perak two years later to replace Birch who was murdered, Douglas took over as British Resident in Selangor.

However, Douglas' performance was below par and he was asked to resign by the Governor in 1882. Frank Swettenham was sent to replace Douglas in August 1882 and he shifted into the wooden Residency which had a dining room, a drawing room, six bedrooms with verandahs and five bathrooms. The floor was made of cement and there were no mats or carpets. Swettenham wrote to Weld that he needed $1,500 for furniture and another $100 annually for maintenance.

While he felt that the Residency was adequate for Douglas, it seemed likely that he thought it unfit for himself.

In 1885, Hugh Low, who was the second British Resident of Perak, went on leave and Swettenham was requested to take over his post temporarily. In Perak, he found the time to draw plans for a new Residency in Kuala Lumpur with the help of the Perak State engineer.

When he returned to Kuala Lumpur, he handed the plan to the Selangor State engineer and asked him to prepare new plans which he sent to the Governor in Singapore, along with a proposal to build the new Residency with Selangor Government funds.

The plans, with some amendments including pillars in the drawing room and a large metal porch, were accepted and the Residency was built near the old structure. Swettenham went on leave from 1886 till 1887 and in his absence, J.P. Rodger took over his post. Construction of the Residency during Rodger's time **A snail's pace ...** continued, but at a snail's pace.

When Swettenham returned to Kuala Lumpur in late 1888, it was still incomplete and he quickly arranged for more workers to finish the job. The Residency was finally completed in 1889, but by then Swettenham was appointed Resident of Perak, a post he held till 1896.

The Residency that Swettenham built was first occupied by his successor, William Maxwell. And when he served as Resident-General of the Federated Malay States till he took up the post of Governor of Singapore in 1901, his residence was the other, much grander, house that he built—Carcosa.

Leading Residents

The last colonial official to live at the Residency was F.V. Dick Duckworth, who served as the last British Adviser in Selangor from 1954 till May 1956. Three months later, Tunku Abdul Rahman, who had become Malaya's Chief Minister, moved in and lived there till he resigned as Prime Minister of Malaysia in 1971.

Thus the Residency has the distinction of having been the residence of the first British Resident, the first Chief Minister and the first Prime Minister of Malaysia.

In 1971, there were plans to demolish the building, but Tunku appealed to the authorities to save it and in 1978, he expressed his wish to see it used as a monument.

His wish was granted on 10 November 1994, when the Residency was reopened as the Tunku Abdul Rahman

Memorial. It was refurbished at a cost of RM32 million with two new wings added to it.

The memorial has about 100,000 exhibits, some dating from 1963. Furniture from Tunku's house in Penang and Kuala Lumpur have been placed in the memorial along with his cigars, spectacles, trophies, medals, awards, photographs and other personal effects.

Furniture from Tunku's office when he was Prime Minister are also on exhibition. There is also a carving in black granite of Tunku with his right hand up in the familiar pose when he shouted 'Merdeka!' An entire section features cartoons and caricatures of Tunku.

The visitor will discover some interesting facets about Tunku—that he was involved in the movies, as director of *Sumpahan Mahsuri* and scriptwriter of *Raja Bersiong*. And also that he liked dancing—Cinta Sayang, which was his favourite, Ronggeng and Mak Inang.

The Residency itself is famed for the sitting room called Cairo Room, named thus because the furniture was bought by Tunku in Cairo (actually, they are replicas made by the Prisons Department and the originals are in his Petaling Jaya house). The Cairo Room was where he received guests. There was a smaller sitting room for his family.

The dining room is also historic, as many decisions of great importance were decided there during Cabinet meetings over some refreshments.

When Tunku became Chief Minister in August 1955, he was offered a house at No. 1, Hose Road, near today's Dewan Bahasa dan Pustaka, but that house was in a poor state. It seems that he was then offered Carcosa, but he preferred the Residency at Brockman Road (renamed Jalan Dato Onn in 1963).

The two-storeyed Residency had five bedrooms, two sitting rooms and a dining room. There were paintings of Tunku and Sharifah Rodziah by Georgette Chen in the Residency.

Tunku also kept pets—two Siamese fighting fish and an Alsatian dog called Seri.

His office was in a single-storeyed wooden building near the tennis court and he simply walked to work, returning to have lunch with his family whenever he could, after which he napped in an air-conditioned bedroom after setting the alarm on his wristwatch.

Tunku had four houseboys who had to wear Malay clothes with scarlet *samping* and black *songket*. He had a personal valet and two drivers. As Prime Minister, he had the choice of using either a Chrysler Imperial or a Cadillac convertible.

Tunku, being the amiable person that he was, was as informal with his staff as he was with others, regardless of their station in life. In 1956, when the visiting Duke of Edinburgh, Prince Philip, was staying at the Residency, he and Tunku searched for durians in the kitchen of the Residency. Tunku must have been trying to introduce the tropical delight to the prince, since no visit would be complete without sampling the king of fruits. It was not recorded, however, whether they found any.

A CLOSER LOOK ...

At the Lake Gardens, it is quite a calming experience to take a walk in one of the few green lungs left in KL, amidst some very ancient trees. Personally, I have a liking for the Orchid Garden and the Bird Park which are unique and well maintained. The air smells sweeter, despite the busy highways and thoroughfares nearby. In the evenings and weekends, joggers throng the running tracks and outdoor exercise stations and families can be seen on outings.

Although the amount of air pollution in KL would render an attempt at combing the night sky at the National Planetarium futile, the special movies there are worth watching. The National Monument, however, is worth visiting both for itself and the stimulating sculptures by Southeast Asian artists at the base of the hill.

The Bangsar Area

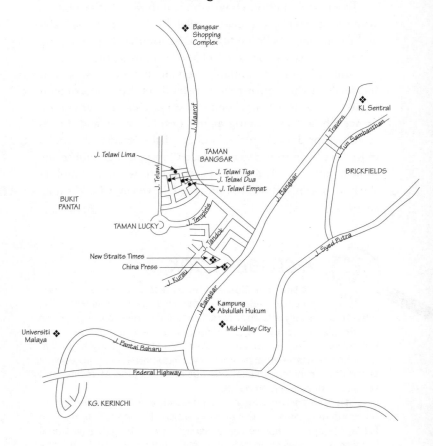

Mostly Millionaires

Bangsar

*How an old rubber estate was turned into
the trendiest place to be...*

How many millionaires are there in Bangsar? As many as there are bungalows in the prime residential area.

The old rubber estate started by investors Bunge and Grisar (the Bungsar road was named after them), which was at one time malaria-infested, has become what a top government official labelled an 'urban slum'.

But urban slum or otherwise, Bangsar is one of the most sought-after addresses in modern day Kuala Lumpur because of its location—within the city's boundaries and minutes away by car to Petaling Jaya.

Bungsar Road was built around 1912 and it was linked to the road which led to the emerging town of Kuala Lumpur. The rubber estate was surrounded by jungle. Over the years, the spelling of Bangsar evolved with an 'a' replacing the 'u'.

The rubber trees have long been felled to make way for single-storeyed and double-storeyed link houses and bungalows. For a long time, Jalan Maarof, the main access road to Bangsar homes, was not linked to Damansara and the housing estate was relatively quiet.

City by the River

Bounded by Jalan Bangsar, Jalan Syed Putra and the Federal Highway, Mid-Valley City will be on the last great patch of wasteland in the city.

It will be a huge RM2.3 billion project, the second largest in Malaysia, on 50 acres of land beside the Klang River. It is a joint venture between City Hall and Mid Valley City Sdn Bhd, a subsidiary of public-listed IGB Corporation Bhd.

To be completed in several phases over 10 years, the entire project will comprise 18 million square feet of integrated development including 16,000 car park bays. Phase One features a five-storeyed Mega Mall with 4.5 million square feet of retail space featuring three major anchor tenants, several mini anchor tenants, about 500 retail outlets and 400,000 square feet of indoor entertainment space. It is the largest retail centre in Asia, and opened just before Christmas in 1999. Along with it will be six office towers, 30 signature offices and a four-star Traders' Hotel, all scheduled to be completed in 1998. In late 1999, only one component of the project had been completed—the Mega Mall.

Phase Two will feature more office towers, hotels and an International Convention Centre.

To make way for Mid-Valley City, one of the oldest kampungs in the city, Kampung Haji Abdullah Hukum, will be demolished and the villagers have already been given new flats to live in.

The kampung was named after its first *penghulu* who settled there with his Kerinchi followers. They cleared the jungle and planted padi, maize and vegetables.

The area in the days of Haji Abdullah Hukum was called Sungei Putih (White River).

Then came the condominium craze and up went the buildings one by one. Now, Bangsar has probably the highest concentration of high-rise upmarket condominiums in the city. It is getting congested, but people still want to live there.

With the ever-growing demand for Bangsar homes, property prices have shot up and now a double-storeyed link house is worth half a million ringgit and a single-storeyed bungalow costs more than a million. Double-storeyed bungalows with big plots of land can fetch more than two million ringgit. Bangsar has created many millionaires in the past few years.

With the affluent Pantai Hills area adjoining Bangsar, the area probably has the highest number of millionaires in the city.

Bangsar is the kind of place that is ever-evolving—there are now two shopping complexes, the Mun Loong outlet next to Bangsar mosque, and the Bangsar Shopping Complex along Jalan Maarof.

Jalan Maarof itself has changed, with many of the bungalows along it being converted into shops selling antiques, lights, furniture and interior decor items.

Settling in White River

The first settlers of Bangsar were not millionaires or yuppies, but a motley group of Kerinchi Malays led by Haji Abdullah Hukum bin Abdul Rahim (1835–1943).

Haji Abdullah Hukum, who sailed to Malaya around 1850 from Kerinchi in Sumatra, founded the kampung in the 1890s.

The able leader managed to obtain permission from the British Resident, William Maxwell (who took over from Swettenham in 1889), and Raja Laut to develop the land in the Sungei Putih area. He had earlier opened farms in the areas now called Bukit Bintang and Bukit Nanas.

With his loyal following of fellow Kerinchis, he settled at White River, cleared the jungle and started farms growing vegetables and fruits.

Bangsar has also become an entertainment district of sorts. Some years back, hawker stalls lined Jalan Telawi Lima and nightbirds and disco-kakis used to pop over for late-night *teh tarik, roti canai* and *nasi lemak*. These were relocated in a building which is fondly known as the Jolly Green Giant. A side road nearby is still lined with stalls every night.

A seafood restaurant proved popular and other restaurants opened. Of late, Bangsar has become very cosmopolitan as expatriate workers and foreign investors have set up homes there.

Now, there are restaurants selling Thai, Turkish, Austrian, Continental, Chinese, Japanese, North Indian, vegetarian, Mexican, Italian and Malaysian food. One can have sushi, laksa, naan, nachos or pizza. Fast-food outlets, ice cream parlours and gourmet coffee joints have also set up shop there. Clubs, pubs and bars have opened next to each other, all trying to outdo each other in terms of concept and decor. The latest fad is the cyber cafe where one can surf the Internet while munching chocolate muffins and drinking coffee. During the recession, many of these cyber cafes closed. Many other outlets also closed or were sold out to investors who still had the guts—and cash.

Despite the recession, trendy Bangsar is still setting the style and pace for the rest of Kuala Lumpur.

Werewolves in KL?

If a local legend is to be believed, Kuala Lumpur had its fair share of roaming werewolves. They apparently strayed into the city from Kampung Kerinchi, which is near Bangsar.

Kampung Kerinchi, situated beside the Federal Highway near Universiti Malaya and the affluent Pantai Hills, was founded by a group of Sumatrans from Kerinchi in the Jambi district of Sumatra in the 1890s.

They were probably linked to the other group of Kerinchi people who founded nearby Kampung Abdullah Hukum.

These Sumatrans had set foot on Malayan soil as early as the 1850s. They settled in Bukit Nanas and Sungei Besi, and grew pineapples. Later, they moved on and ended up founding Kampung Kerinchi where they cleared land and cultivated vegetables, fruits and padi. Some of the kampung folk were reputed to have the power to turn themselves into wolves. ·

The kampung folk used to sell their vegetables and fruits at Central Market and it was a four-hour trek to get to the town centre. Some people still recall waking up at 3 am to hike on jungle paths to get to Kuala Lumpur's main market at Rodger Street.

Kampung Kerinchi today is like a modern suburb with low-cost flats and new apartment blocks. It is connected by a new road to numerous blocks of condominiums at the adjoining Pantai Panorama hilltop project.

Old News

New Straits Times Press Group
Jalan Riong

The Malay Mail comes after dessert.

The Malay Mail, the afternoon English tabloid which has become synonymous with charitable activities, turned 100 in 1996.

The newspaper—an indispensable guide for job seekers and those who want to pick up a second-hand car because of its popular Classifieds section—has become an institution in Kuala Lumpur. Reading it while having lunch has become a habit for many residents in the Klang Valley. After the menu, *The Malay Mail* is next.

The Malay Mail was Kuala Lumpur's first newspaper when it was launched on 14 December 1896 by John H.M. Robson, the son of a clergyman who started his sojourn in the East as a tea planter in Ceylon at the age of 19.

Though Robson was a newspaper publisher, he apparently did not have journalism in his blood. Years later, he wrote: 'If I had my time over again I should have no desire whatsoever to start a daily newspaper in Malaya or elsewhere.'

Before *The Malay Mail*, which was a broadsheet then, there were other publications. In 1890, the Selangor Government published its official *Selangor Gazette*, which was somewhat like a newsletter that included local news and advertisements. In 1892, the *Selangor Journal* was launched by the Government printer and two men—Robson and W.W. Skeat.

A magazine which contained local and foreign news, snippets of gossip on European life in Kuala Lumpur and

Selangor, historical articles and personal perspectives, the gazette lasted four years till the launch of *The Malay Mail*.

In those days, the newspaper was very different from today's editions. The front page comprised advertisements on property for sale, services available and shipping available.

The first issue had advertisers such as Chow Kit & Co; Macreath's The Dispensary; A.C. Harper & Co; Chartered Bank of India, Australia and China; Riley, Hargreaves & Co; The Straits Trading Company Limited; Boustead & Co and Howarth Erskine Limited. Several mare and pony harnesses were also advertised for sale.

From a shophouse at Market Street, Robson more or less single-handedly wrote, edited, solicited for advertisements and printed the four-paged (its pagination increased to 16 later) *The Malay Mail*, which had a circulation of 200.

The Malay Mail is now owned by the New Straits Times Press Group, Malaysia's largest newspaper publisher.

The Old Faithful

The *New Straits Times*, an institution in Malaysian journalism, started off as *The Straits Times* and *Singapore Journal of Commerce*. It commenced publication on 15 July 1845, from a small shoplot at No. 7, Commercial Square (today known as Raffles Place), Singapore.

It was 'printed on new types, on fine English paper' and consisted of eight folio papers. It cost half a Spanish dollar per copy.

It was not the first newspaper to be printed in this part of the world—the *Singapore Chronicle* was first published in 1824 and the *Singapore Free Press* in 1835. There was a third newspaper, called *Straits Messenger*, which was published before *The Straits Times* and the *Singapore Journal of Commerce*. But all these have disappeared from the scene.

The Straits Times and *Singapore Journal of Commerce*, founded by Martenius Thaddens Apcar and edited by Robert Carr Woods, were not so much newspapers, but weekly newsletters, published on Tuesdays, for traders and shippers.

'The arrangements made by the Proprietor will, it is confidently expected, ensure for *The Straits Times* a wide circulation, especially amongst the mercantile community, whilst the principles on which the publication will be conducted are those which will ever identify *The Straits Times* with the general interests of the Settlement,' stated the front-page announcement on the first edition of the newspaper, which sounded almost like a mission statement.

The front page comprised mainly advertisements on shipping schedules of vessels heading for destinations like Batavia, London, Manila and Calcutta. There were also advertisements for the sale of 'a few boxes of fresh Japanese rice', 'an excellent billiard table with cues, bridges, apparatus for lamps', 'two Guzerat Milch goats with three kids: all in excellent condition', and a 'comfortable and conveniently situated house in High Street, suitable for a family with out-house complete'.

There were large advertisements on the sale of a 'valuable and choice selection of British, French and China goods' at the Cursetjee & Co shop at Commercial Square and the efficaciousness of Holloway's Pills and Ointment which were 'innocuous to the tenderest infant or to the weakest constitution, and equally prompt and sure in eradicating disease from the most robust frame'.

High-Flying Antics

When the *New Straits Times* (NST) celebrated its 150th anniversary in 1995, the newspaper organised an international hot air balloon festival. It was launched with the high fliers of NST, the Information Minister, Datuk Mohamed Rahmat, and the Datuk Bandar (mayor), Datuk Mazlan Ahmad, taking a ride on one of the balloons at Merdeka Square. They reached a height of 45.7 metres and had a good view of the KL skyline.

The hot air balloonfest saw some 20 brightly-coloured balloons from Britain and other European countries taking to the skies of Kuala Lumpur and other cities in Malaysia.

It was the first time many KL residents had seen a hot air balloon, but not the first time that one had graced KL's sky. If they had been around a century ago, they would have seen a hot air balloon 'flying' in Kuala Lumpur.

In 1894, Professor Lawrence who styled himself as a 'Practical Aeronaut and Aerial Engineer' made his way to Kuala Lumpur (it is not recorded whether he arrived by his hot air balloon or by normal means of transportation) and prepared to take a flight in 'a balloon inflated with hot air from a fire laced with paraffin' at the Padang in front of Selangor Club. Apparently, it was done for a fee and initially, there were some problems raising the minimum amount, but when a Chinese spectator offered to underwrite the event, Prof Lawrence gamely took to flight.

The *Selangor Journal* reported: 'He then moved off to the parachute, while a local sportsman dashed through the crowd with a bottle of beer wherewith to refresh him, took leave of his colleagues, bade farewell to his wife, ordered the stays to be cast loose, and, amidst enthusiastic clapping and cheering, the balloon slowly soared aloft to a height of 20 feet (6 metres).'

The newspaper catered to readers in the Straits Settlements and there was a monthly summary consisting of eight pages 'comprising a precis of intelligence connected with the Straits China' which was despatched by steamer to Europe.

In 1858, it became a daily newspaper with more emphasis on local news. A Saturday weekly edition was also published for its overseas readers, especially in Malacca and Penang. Even though it was the leading newspaper of the region then, its circulation was not more than 200 for the first 50 years of its publication.

The newspaper has been published everyday without fail, except for a three and a half year break during World War II.

In 1972, the newspaper split into two separate entities—the Singaporean *The Straits Times* and the Malaysian *New Straits Times*. In both countries the newspapers became the leading and most influential publications (Although *The Star* has somewhat overtaken the *New Straits Times* in recent years).

In the old days, the newspaper's office in Kuala Lumpur was at Jalan Pudu near Bukit Bintang. It later shifted to 31, Jalan Riong, Bangsar.

A CLOSER LOOK ...

At Bangsar, this suburb is ever-changing and if you want to have a taste of the really trendy nightlife of KL, this is the place to be.

J. Telawi Tiga has the reputation of being the street with the most clubs and pubs in Malaysia. Prices are on the steep side but, since the trendies drive to Bangsar in Mercedes Benzs and BMWs, they don't complain and the owners of the watering holes don't either. The attitude here is—if you can't afford Bangsar prices, you are perhaps in the wrong part of town. Even the hawkers are pricier, but it is still cheaper to line your stomach with a *roti canai* or two than to order a plate of fried potato skin or some other 'sophisticated' thing.

Most of the nightspots and clubs are located along J. Telawi Dua or J. Telawi Tiga. During special occasions like Christmas Eve or New Year's Eve, the roads are car-free, and pedestrians plus party animals invade the streets by the thousands.

The seafood restaurants (along J. Telawi Dua) are still popular although more affordable food can be found at the Jolly Green Giant or at the hawker stalls outside. It is something like a KL swinger's tradition to have a great time in the city and end up in Bangsar for *teh tarik* and *roti canai* in the wee hours of the morning. The hawkers aren't complaining.

The Bukit Bintang Area

Starry, Starry Hill

Bukit Bintang

*People grew up fast on the tough
streets of Star Hill.*

Young girls living in Bukit Bintang learnt at an early age not to wear cheongsams, hold their hankies daintily nor ride on trishaws. For that was the signature of the strumpets of Star Hill (Bukit Bintang in Malay).

Chow Kit had its share of prostitutes, but they were predominantly Malay. Bukit Bintang was the pleasure dome for the Chinese. Not only were many of the women there streetwalkers, but some were kept women. Rich Chinese towkays had the habit of stashing their mistresses in Bukit Bintang flats.

Of course, today's hookers do not wave little hankies or ride trishaws any more. These days, pimps in Proton Wiras filled with well-dressed, good-looking girls drive around the area, park outside Sun Complex (reputed to have several apartments which are centres of nefarious activities) and communicate with each other and their mamasans (normally oldish women who are in charge of these outlets of sexual pleasure) with digital GSM handphones. It is a bit more sophisticated and hi-tech these days.

*Hi-tech
mama-sans ...*

Bukit Bintang has two faces—one segment of it, closer to Jalan Raja Chulan (previously known as Weld Road), is more residential and genteel while the other segment, closer to Jalan Bukit Bintang and Jalan Imbi, is rough and rowdy. That is where the dark side of Bukit Bintang lurks and, of course, where the crowds are.

The genteel part has bungalows and posh apartments especially near the Jalan Bukit Ceylon area where several luxurious condominiums have been built in the past few years. The other side of Bukit Bintang has shophouses, offices and cheaper flats.

In the old days, Bukit Bintang was where one could dance the night away at the famed BB Park, an amusement centre which over the years became rather ramshackle but offered lots of fun and excitement anyway.

BB Park had something for everyone. Old-timers will recall the dance girls dressed in cheongsams and sarong kebayas. In the 1950s, it cost 20 cents for a round of Ronggeng on an open-air platform while inside an enclosed hall, one could fox-trot or cha-cha with the girls at 25 cents per dance.

BB Park had lots of stalls selling food, drinks, garments and souvenirs. One could win prizes at game stalls by knocking down a wall of tin cans with a certain number of balls; aiming a dart at the right playing card; or throwing a ball into a cut-out clown's mouth.

There were roller coaster rides, a Ferris wheel, merry-go-round, dodgem cars and slot machines. There were also peep holes where those in the know, mostly naughty children from the neighbourhood, could find out what was happening behind closed curtains.

The games stalls and fun-rides were at the front portion of BB Park while the rear portion presented a warren of crumbling cubicles where prostitutes would do a trick for $8 back in the 1960s.

BB Park was also notorious for gang wars and inside the amusement park itself were several gangs, each controlling a section of it. Turf wars were common.

In the 1930s, Bukit Bintang contained only three mansions, a Chinese school, the Bukit Bintang Girls' School, a few churches and several orchards growing rambutans and durians. In the old days, it was also known as Bukit Kopi or Kopi San ('Coffee Hill' in Malay and Cantonese respectively) because coffee was grown in the area.

In the later part of the 19th century, Bukit Bintang was settled by Kerinchi Malays who were led by Haji Abdullah Hukum. They opened farms and grew vegetables, sugar cane, bananas, sirih and fruits.

Money River

In the 1930s, a tiger was spotted strolling down the middle of Jalan Bukit Bintang heading towards Pudu. At that time (and even now), Pudu was called Poon San Pa ('half jungle' in Cantonese).

Later, more buildings and shophouses were built in the area. The tallest at one time was the four-storeyed Capitol Hotel owned by property tycoon, Tan Sri Low Yat.

In the late 1950s, the 21-storeyed Federal Hotel, also built by Tan Sri Low Yat, became the tallest building and the earliest luxury hotel in the city. The hotel, upgraded over the years, is still operating today and its top-floor revolving restaurant, which was its star attraction back then, is still drawing in the crowds.

Children who grew up in Bukit Bintang would remember clambering all over to catch a glimpse of Hong Kong movie stars who would grace events at Pavilion cinema and Federal Hotel.

The First Luxury Hotel

The Federal Hotel in Bukit Bintang was the first international-standard hotel in Malaya. Tunku Abdul Rahman asked contractor (later Tan Sri) Low Yat to build the hotel to house guests for the Independence Day celebrations. Low Yat summoned his son, Low Yow Chuan (now Tan Sri), who was then studying architecture in Australia, to return home and help plan the hotel which was completed in time for the celebrations on 31 August 1957.

Tan Sri Low Yow Chuan was reported as saying: 'Tunku used to treat the Federal Hotel like his own. Most Government functions were held there. We were the only grand hotel then. The Merlin came later. Everybody came. It was packed every night. There were not many tourists those days, so those who came were mostly local people.'

Some years back, the metal cladding on the ceiling of the overhang at the hotel's entrance collapsed and broke three of the four stone lions guarding the front doors. These were quickly replaced and word spread around town that Datuk Low Yow Chuan had lady luck on his side as the fourth guardian lion was spared and there was still good *feng shui* flowing into his hotel.

Federal was the grandest hotel in Kuala Lumpur in the late 1950s and it was matched only when the Merlin Hotel (now called Concord Hotel), at the junction of Jalan Ampang and Jalan Sultan Ismail, was built in 1959.

Today's Bukit Bintang is one of the busiest spots in the city with a large number of shopping complexes. The old BB Park has been demolished and rebuilt on its site is Sungei Wang ('Money River' in Malay, but its Chinese name means 'Gold River') Plaza. Upgraded several times, the shopping complex, which celebrated its 20th anniversary in 1997, has become an institution in the retail trade and is still the most popular shopping centre in the city.

Star City

Newspapers called it 'A Star In The Making' when earthworks for the project started in 1995. The Berjaya Star City project, located at the edge of Bukit Bintang at the junction of Jalan Imbi and Jalan Pudu, is another of Kuala Lumpur's mega projects.

The Berjaya Star City will have two million square feet of retail space, 1 million square feet of leisure/entertainment space, 1.5 million square feet of service suites and a total of 4,768 parking bays.

It will have two anchor tenants, 30 mini anchor tenants and 900 shops. The building will also house two indoor theme parks—Asia's largest water theme park and another entertainment theme park which will feature Asia's longest indoor roller coaster.

There will also be 12 cineplexes, a 48-lane bowling alley, an ice-skating rink and a 4,000-seat theatre restaurant.

It will have a 16-storeyed shopping complex and two 45-storeyed tower blocks of service suites.

The RM2 billion Berjaya Star City is to be built on 5.2 hectares of land. Due for completion in 1998, work on it is still progressing.

Monthly, 2.2 million people go to Sungei Wang Plaza, which has two department stores—Parkson Grand and Metro—and hundreds of smaller shops and a couple of cineplexes. Adjoining Sungei Wang is Bukit Bintang Plaza. Fronting Jalan Imbi near Sungei Wang Plaza is Imbi Plaza.

Opposite Sungei Wang is Lot 10, a modern shopping complex which was built on the site of the old Bukit Bintang Dance Hall and wet market. Lot 10 is more upmarket and has Isetan as its anchor tenant. It is linked to the front of Sungei Wang by an overhead pedestrian bridge.

A few blocks behind Lot 10 is the newest shopping complex in the area—Star Hill Centre. This impressive shopping place has leading Singaporean retailer Tangs, as its anchor tenant. Adjoining Star Hill Centre is the posh J.W. Marriott hotel. Behind it, along Jalan Imbi, the exclusive Ritz-Carlton hotel has opened.

Beside Star Hill Centre is KL Plaza, another shopping complex, which has been boosted by crowd-pulling new tenants like Tower Records, Planet Hollywood and fancy coffee joints like Starbucks and Coffee Bean.

One can check out the elite designer boutiques at Star Hill Centre and walk out of the shopping complex only to be offered pirated versions of the exact same thing. Bukit Bintang offers shopping opportunities to suit any budget. A Gucci belt could cost between RM300 and RM400 inside Star Hill and only from RM30 to RM40 outside.

Bukit Bintang also has a large number of hotels. Behind Federal Hotel is the Melia, which used to be the Prince. Opposite Sungei Wang Plaza is the Park Royal, formerly known as the Regent. The Regent shifted to a newer building opposite KL Plaza.

The McDonald's outlet at Bukit Bintang was the first to open in Malaysia. In the old days, there were a couple of massage parlours next door to McDonald's. These closed when rental and property values shot up in recent years. Even residential buildings have been converted into shops, showrooms and offices. Old bungalows have been demolished to make way for skyscrapers.

Bukit Bintang is now promoted as a shopping paradise. It is within walking distance of five-star hotels such as the Kuala Lumpur Hilton, Istana and Ritz-Carlton. Energetic guests from Shangri-La, Concord, Holiday Inn On The Park and Equatorial hotel can also walk to the bright lights of Bukit Bintang.

The Cost of Education

Bukit Bintang Girls' School, one of the most outstanding schools in Kuala Lumpur, is just like Pudu Jail—only in the sense that the city grew around it. Today, it is surrounded by the Regent Hotel, Star Hill and KL Plaza shopping centres.

From the educationist's point of view, all these attractions (or distractions) plus the din of traffic and pollution would not be good for the students. From the businessman's point of view, however, the old school is sitting on prime land, which could be redeveloped for a large profit.

Bukit Bintang Girls' school

Nobody is quite sure which point of view won the authorities over, but the school was ordered to shift out of the city centre. In September 1996, it was announced that a consortium comprising Syarikat Usaha Harta Cemerlang Sdn Bhd, Syarikat Tanah dan Harta Sdn Bhd and Syarikat Urus Harta Sdn Bhd would be building a RM144.5 million educational complex on 12.5 hectares of land in Pudu Ulu Cheras. This complex will house four Smart Schools where selected children will be sent for special education geared towards information technology, motivating them to be creative and innovative. A new building for Bukit Bintang Girls' School (it is uncertain if the name will be retained) will also be built.

In exchange, the consortium will be given the right to redevelop the prime land where the existing Bukit Bintang Girls' School is situated. The consortium plans to build a RM1 billion commercial complex which is likely to include apartments, hotels, eateries, retail and entertainment outlets.

Bukit Bintang Girls' School has a proud tradition of academic excellence. The school was founded by Christian missionaries in 1893 and it was then known as the Chinese Girls' School and was located in Brickfields.

Later, it moved to Davidson Road and in 1930, it shifted to its present site in Bukit Bintang.

The founder, Miss Betty Langlands, assumed the name of Mrs J.W. Moore upon marriage. The first headmistress was Miss Bessie Maclay who arrived in Kuala Lumpur from China in 1895 to teach scripture.

She was credited with setting the high standards of discipline and academic performance which have been perpetuated by succeeding headmistresses.

Miss Maclay had a good heart and was known for hiring rickshas to take poor children to Sunday School. She operated a dispensary at her home. When unwanted babies were left at her doorstep, she ended up taking care of five children.

Another headmistress who was fondly remembered was Miss Eva Prouse, who had one wing of the school named after her. Miss Prouse died in a Japanese prison camp in Palembang in February, 1945 and she left all her savings to her beloved BBGS.

Ex-students of BBGS hope that such sacrifices will not be forgotten in the name of progress.

The 72-Storeyed Bus Station

A clubhouse, in a half-timber mock-Tudor style, used to stand along Jalan Pudu—the Selangor Chinese Recreation Club (SCRC).

The clubhouse, somewhat reminiscent of Selangor Club, was opened in 1930. This club had been in existence some years before and had occupied a shophouse at Pudu Road.

The SCRC, often called the Chinese Minstrels, was famed for its high-calibre footballers; and the club produced some famous players like Soh Chin Aun, Wong Choon Wah and Lim Fung Kee. Its prowess in football dates back to as early as 1926 to 1928 when it was the FA Cup champion for three years.

But SCRC members pursued other interests too, such as billiards and chess. The billiard tables were as old as the clubhouse.

During World War II, the Japanese used the clubhouse as the headquarters of its army transport unit, while Japanese soldiers turned the field into their camp.

In 1995, the field became a huge hole, dug up for the foundation of a project undertaken by Plaza Rakyat Sdn Bhd, a subsidiary of public-listed Wembley Industries Holding Berhad.

The project, called Plaza Rakyat, was budgeted at RM2 billion and was originally scheduled for completion in 1998. Work on it has stalled.

The project will be a main transport terminus connecting the LRT to a bus and taxi station. It will replace the existing Puduraya as a transportation terminus and reduce traffic congestion in that busy area.

Plaza Rakyat will comprise a 72-storeyed office block, an LRT station, a bus terminal, a 470-room four-star hotel, a 157-room budget hotel, 300 service apartments and 3,000 parking bays. There will be a shopping plaza with 1.1 million square feet of retail space.

The existing Puduraya building will be demolished to make way for a park with an underground (somewhat like Dataran Merdeka) shopping and recreation centre.

The SCRC has shifted to new premises in Pandan Jaya.

Fish Curry with Rice?

Pudu Jail, Jalan Hang Tuah

*If the walls of Pudu Jail could talk,
it would be a tall tale.*

It sounds too incredible to be true, but Gullick recorded it. In the early days, Pudu Jail actually had three European warders whose surnames were Fish, Currie and Rice.

It is an old joke that prisoners were served curry and rice on the government's account.

In Pudu Jail, not only did warders have spicy names, but at least one had a name which sounded somewhat like his job specialisation. Indeed, there was a Mr Galloway who was in charge of the gallows.

Pudu Jail was located in the centre of the city and could be seen from several five-star hotels, shopping complexes, apartments and the Bankers' Club. The road in front, Jalan Hang Tuah, is rather busy and many a passer-by has commented on the jail, especially its wall which was painted with jungle scenes.

The Art of Crime

The painting on Pudu Jail's wall is possibly Kuala Lumpur's most prominent work of art; yet the artist is uncelebrated.

Pha Tee was serving time in Pudu Jail in the 1980s for possessing stolen goods. He was a drug addict and had been in and out of prison. His first jail term was for robbery in 1963 when he was barely 21.

In 1985, when the prison authorities wanted to brighten up the drab wall of the prison, they decided to give Pha Tee the opportunity to prove himself.

Using a roller and his bare hands, Pha Tee rolled and smeared paint on the wall. He created scenes based on

his memories of places he had visited and photographs he had seen in books and magazines.

His work was a naive view of lush jungle scenery, beach scenes, blue skies, cotton-woolly clouds and flowers. It seemed so innocent that it was hard to believe it was the work of a career criminal.

It was a common sight at that time to see Pha Tee accompanied by a warder painting the wall along Jalan Pudu and Jalan Hang Tuah. Sometimes, several other prisoners helped to splash paint on the wall. In all, some 2,000 litres of paint were used. The painted prison wall is 384 metres long and 5.4 metres tall.

It might seem strange that the largest prison in Kuala Lumpur was in the middle of the city, but when it was completed in 1895, it was at the edge of town beside the rough road that led to tin mines in Pudu. The Cantonese name for Pudu is 'Poon San Pa' which means 'half-jungle', accurately describing the conditions back then. This term is still in use today though the surroundings have become a concrete jungle.

Pudu Jail was built on the site of Pudu Village and two isolated roads—Rathbone Street and Hill Street—were demolished to make way for it.

The jail was built in six phases. First to be put up was the fortress wall in February 1891. Then the administrative building, 240 cells in three-storeyed blocks, hospital and wardens' quarters were erected. Total costs amounted to $138,000.

The first batch of prisoners were from all over Selangor—Jugra, Hulu Langat, Banting, Ampang, Klang and Rawang.

It was reported that while the jail was being constructed in the **Cows in jail...** 1890s, stray cows roamed the area freely and one was not certain whether the wall was built to keep the cows out or the prisoners in.

Hanging in the Balance

Even the prison staff had a healthy sense of humour. A European hangman, when asked whether there was a verdict reached regarding a serious crime case, replied: 'The verdict's not decided. You could say it's hanging in the balance.'

Though Pudu Jail looked aged, it functioned very well. So well, in fact, that it became overcrowded.

No Escape

The modern escape-proof prison replacing Pudu Jail is located at Sungei Buloh—at the edge of today's Kuala Lumpur.

Completed in the middle of 1996 at a cost of RM170 million, the prison has modern features such as anti-tunnelling floors and anti-scaling walls, hi-tech sensors, fibre-optic devices and more comfortable cells. The prison, said to be the most sophisticated in Asia, can hold 2,500 prisoners.

The transfer of prisoners from Pudu Jail to the new jail was delayed for a few months because the contractors had simply buried waste building materials like metal rods and pipes in the inmates' exercise yard instead of throwing them into the garbage dump. They then filled up the yard with earth, covering the rods and pipes, and planted the topsoil with grass. The metallic objects could have been used by the prisoners as weapons and they could have affected the highly-sensitive electronic sensors. In which case, the escape-proof jail could have become a big joke.

The prison authorities had to borrow metal detectors from the army and police to locate and remove these potential weapons.

In a swap deal, the new prison was built by the Urban Development Authority (UDA) on a 48-hectare site in Sungei Buloh in exchange for the right to develop the 8.9-hectare piece of land where Pudu Jail is sited.

UDA will build a mixed-development project comprising condominiums, a shopping complex and a hotel at the site. It will be called Bandar Baru KL II. Detailed plans have yet to be announced.

This development is in line with City Hall's intention to turn the area near the Jalan Imbi-Jalan Hang Tuah-Jalan Pudu intersection into a major shopping area.

Hopefully, UDA will be sensitive to the history of Pudu Jail and at the very least, its unique wall with its child-like painting, which has become a landmark, will be retained. Is there no escape from development?

When it was built, it was designed for 600 prisoners. In the 1980s and 1990s, the number of prisoners exceeded its maximum capacity many times over. At one time, there were as many as 6,000 prisoners and they had to take turns to sleep.

The problem of overcrowding was alleviated somewhat with the completion of a prison in Kajang.

Though tens of thousands of its criminals have committed all sorts of crimes outside its walls, Pudu Jail was once itself the scene of a crime.

In October 1985, two doctors who were treating prisoners, Dr Radzi Jaafar and Dr Abdul Aziz Abdul Majid, were held hostage by six remand prisoners.

The six comprised Jimmy Chuah, the leader, Ng Lai Huat, Sim Ah Lan, Lam Hock Sang, Pang Boon Ho and Yap Chee Keong. The first four faced charges under the Firearms (Increased Penalties) Act. After holding the doctors hostage for six days, they surrendered.

By the end of 1996, Pudu Jail became nothing but a maze of musty buildings filled with painful and poignant memories waiting for the bulldozers to move in. The prisoners had been transferred to an ultra-modern prison in Sungei Buloh and Pudu Jail became the site of another multi-million ringgit mega project.

But the financial crash of 1997 ensured that the old building would remain standing for some time yet. In May 1997, it was opened to the public as an exhibition centre with prison life being its attraction.

People paid to enter the gate and walk along dim and dank corridors, peer into old cells and watch a prison warden demonstrate how caning of prisoners with a thick *rotan* (Malay for 'cane') was carried out. There was also a room which showed how a criminal was hanged. The exhibition was interesting if a bit amateurish, and was viewed by thousands of visitors by the time it closed in late 1998.

Meanwhile, the building itself with its painted walls has slowly evolved into a state of disrepair, with paint peeling off and plants growing in crevices.

An Institution in Education

Victoria Institution
Jalan Hang Tuah

*This school's harsh legacy has ensured that
it will produce students of the same high
calibre year after year...*

Students of the Victoria Institution (VI) were called
'Vagabond Idiots' by their detractors who somehow felt
ruffled by the elitist attitude of the VI guys.

VI has always been regarded as the leading school in Kuala
Lumpur, but it is not the oldest English school.

In 1890, a Government English School was started by the
Reverend Frederick Haines, vicar of the Church of England in
Kuala Lumpur. He combined his post as chaplain with that of
Inspector of Schools, the *de facto* head of education, till 1895.

Meanwhile, the sons of the raja had to be educated away
from the peasants—they went to the Raja School which was
situated somewhere near Gombak Lane close to today's Jalan
Raja, the road having taken its name from the school. Haines
was teaching English at Raja School which had an enrolment
of 11 in 1892—eight sons of Rajas and two sons of sheikhs
plus the Raja Muda of Selangor.

Soon, he realised that having two schools stretched
resources to the limit and it made better sense to merge them.
The residents of Kuala Lumpur were also calling for a better
equipped school.

Treacher, who had just taken over as Resident, found that
some $3,188 collected in 1887 to celebrate Queen Victoria's
Jubilee was not spent and was still listed somewhere in the
1893 accounts.

Treacher used the money for an education fund, adding
another $5,000 from government funds. The Sultan of Selangor
donated $1,100 and the three richest locals of that time—

Kapitan Cina Yap Kwan Seng, State Councillor Loke Yew and Indian leader Thamboosamy Pillai—each contributed over $1,100.

A total of $21,641 was raised which was sufficient to build a new school. Mrs Treacher laid the foundation stone on 14 August 1893. Because of its connection with the Queen Victoria Jubilee fund, the school was called Victoria Institution.

VI's first headmaster Bennett Eyre Shaw, an Oxford scholar, was from the High school, Bishop's Stortford, and he arrived in June 1894. The building at High Street (now called Jalan Tun H.S. Lee) was described as 'picturesque, substantial and suitable'. At that time, the Klang River flowed much nearer to the building and the masters used to amuse themselves shooting crocodiles from the playground.

The Case of the Headmaster's Wife

On 23 April 1911, a woman grabbed a revolver and fired six shots at a man called William Steward. He died almost instantly. Her name was Ethel Proudlock, and she was the wife of the acting headmaster.

In court, her story was that while her husband was not in, William Steward turned up at her house unexpectedly and attempted to rape her.

She said her hand 'came in contact with a revolver' and she shot in self-defence. However, the facts of the case were that she had initially shot him twice and when he tried to run away, she fired another four shots and his body was found a short distance from where she alleged the rape attempt took place.

It was never proven that they were lovers, though it was rumoured that they were, and she admitted that she had met him at Selangor Club the previous day and had invited him to drop by at her house when he was free.

Ethel Proudlock was found guilty of murder.

Gullick said: 'There was evidence of the character, mental and sexual condition of Mrs Proudlock and of Steward which would have rejoiced the heart of the editor of an English Sunday newspaper of the sensational type.

Few could have believed that Mrs Proudlock was innocent but there were many who wished to do so in order to avoid having to admit that a sordid relationship between Europeans had ended in murder.'

There was a petition for a pardon and the power to do so was vested in the Selangor Sultan. The court had recommended that the death sentence be commuted to a jail term. The petition for pardon reached the State Executive Council which was presided by the Sultan who decided to grant the pardon. Mrs Proudlock then left for home in England and nobody knows what happened to her afterwards.

But the story doesn't end there. When renowned writer Somerset Maugham visited Kuala Lumpur in 1922, he stayed with a friend who happened to be Mrs Proudlock's lawyer from whom he learnt about the case and felt that it could be the backbone of a short story.

He wrote *The Letter* which appeared in his *Malayan Short Stories* and it was more or less based on the Ethel Proudlock case. *The Letter* was made into a movie starring Bette Davis.

Gullick added: 'In Somerset Maugham's story, there are two essential differences. The wife is acquitted and there is vital evidence, which would have convicted her— the letter which she wrote to summon her lover to the house. The story is about the recovery and destruction of the letter and the effect of its existence on those who know of it. In particular the husband (in the story he was a planter not a schoolmaster) is prepared to ruin himself to pay for the delivery to him of the letter.'

And thus the case of the headmaster's wife which occurred in some far-flung corner of the Empire became known the world over.

Headmaster on Patrol

The first batch of 198 pupils comprised 104 Chinese, 60 Indians, 24 Eurasians and 10 Malays. Each pupil paid $1 per month.

There were two assistant masters, Mr Buxton and Mr Arudpragasim. Shaw started a tradition of discipline in the school and the rod was not spared. There was a case of a student who was given six of the best for gambling with his school fees. In more recent times, there was the legendary headmaster Murugasu who used to patrol the school not with a walking stick, but a long, thick cane which he put to good use with such frequency that students cowered in fear whenever he walked past.

With these rather convincing methods, aspirations to excel were inculcated in the students.

In 1929, a much larger building with a clock tower was completed on a hill near the original Selangor Golf Club and the school shifted there. That building at Jalan Hang Tuah (formerly called Shaw Road), which was designed by A.C. Norman, has been declared a heritage school and though not as elitist as before, the school still commands respect.

The institution scored firsts in many things—it was the first to start a prefect system in 1923, it was converted into the first secondary school in 1929 and the first to start science classes in 1930 and the first to have a swimming pool. Its 1st Selangor Scout Group (later called 1st KL and now 1st Bukit Bintang) was the oldest scout group in the country.

During World War II, the Japanese used VI as their camp and rumour has it that it was a torture chamber too. When the war ended, the Japanese formally surrendered at the school on 12 September 1945.

A torture chamber in school ...

The original Victoria Institution is still standing right next to the police station at Jalan Tun H.S. Lee, but the Klang river now flows much further away and there are no crocodiles left to shoot. The building is no longer used as a school; it is a drama centre.

The Saints March In

In 1906, the Roman Catholic missionaries founded the St. John's Institution, and ever since then, the Johanians have been the arch-enemies of the Vagabond Idiots. Students of these old, established schools are fiercely loyal to their alma maters even though they may now be in their 40s or 50s, some relaxing in their retirement.

St. John's Institution is housed in an impressive building atop Bukit Nanas next to Convent Bukit Nanas, another old school. When the building was being constructed, there were lots of delays because tigers often attacked the oxen pulling building materials up the thickly-forested hill. The building was completed in 1907.

The Malaysian Eiffel

KL Tower

Jalan Raja Chulan

On a clear day, you cannot see forever...

The KL Tower—a symbol of national pride.

Bukit Nanas is about the only green lung left in KL. A
century ago, it was the site of the fort built by Sutan
Puasa, one of the early settlers and Malay headman of
the mining town.

Now, the hill has a different kind of citadel in the form of
a tower. Instead of influencing events with muskets and
cannons, it now exerts its power with the new weapon of the
20th century—telecommunications.

At 421 metres, the pretty pink Kuala Lumpur Tower is the fourth tallest in the world, losing out to the Toronto CN Tower at 553 metres, the Moscow Ostankino Tower at 537 metres and the Oriental Pearl Television Tower in Shanghai, completed in May 1995, which is 468 metres tall.

It is one of the three tall structures that make the KL skyline easily recognisable. The other two are the Petronas Towers.

Built at the fringe of a forest reserve, the KL Tower, which is as tall as an 85-storeyed building, utilised German technology. In fact, the German builder Wayss and Freytag is also co-owner of the structure with partner Telekom Enterprise, a subsidiary of Telekoms Malaysia.

A Vic-Tree for Greenies

Before the KL Tower was built, the Forestry Department made it very clear that not too many trees could be felled.

When a 150-year-old Jelutong tree was found to be in the way of the project, the planners had to work around it.

The tree was right at the edge of the 20-metre deep pit dug for the tower's foundation. Some parts of the roots had to be cut, but much of the root system was left intact. A special retaining wall was built to prevent the tree from toppling into the pit and other measures were used to ensure that the tree did not lean. It was also watered every day for the entire duration of the three-year construction. The aged tree survived the stress.

Accountants worked out the cost of the entire exercise—it was half a million ringgit.

Marketed as the Malaysian Eiffel Tower, it has attractions like a revolving restaurant on the second floor of the six-storeyed tower head and a public observatory, complete with binoculars and telescopes, on the first floor. Of course, there are souvenir shops selling Malaysian collectibles.

Another attraction is decidedly American—McDonald's.

The fast-food outlet at KL Tower has the distinction of being the highest McDonald's eatery in the world. And it has added a special item on the menu—the Tower Burger.

The upper floors are utilised by Telekom for its analogue and digital telecommunication facilities and Radio Televisyen Malaysia (RTM), the government radio and television network. RTM's new channel, featuring sports events, was planned to be broadcast from the tower. The Meteorological Department occupies the top floor.

On a clear day, though you cannot see forever, you can see as far as the Straits of Malacca.

Built at a cost of RM270 million, the tower also features a theatre, shops and a prayer room. At its base, there are 110 parking bays for cars and five for tourist coaches. The lobby has Islamic decorations in the form of calligraphy and motifs which are the work of eight artists from Isfahan, Iran, who were sent to spruce up the tower after Isfahan was twinned with Kuala Lumpur.

The KL Tower, which weighs an estimated 100,000 tonnes, was built on 4.4 hectares of land and since it is at the edge of the Bukit Nanas forest reserve, the builders had to ensure that as few trees as possible were felled for the project.

Construction started in 1992 and it opened officially in late 1996. When construction began, it was to be the third tallest tower in the world, but before it could be completed, the tower in Shanghai was already erected. The KL Tower is featured in the new RM2 currency note, which was released just before the double Chinese New Year and Hari Raya Aidil Fitri festivals at the beginning of 1996.

A CLOSER LOOK ...

At Bukit Bintang, though it is one of the red-light districts in KL, it is still pretty safe, even at night. And the good-time girls are around, if you know where to find them. Chances are, however, you will be in this area for the shopping opportunities offered by Sungei Wang Plaza, Bukit Bintang Plaza, Lot 10 and Starhill. Although the beautiful Suria KLCC (at the base of the Petronas Twin Towers at J. Ampang) have lured quite a number of the shoppers and big-name labels away, Sungei Wang is always crowded and things are still slightly cheaper there. Isetan at Lot 10 and Tangs at Starhill are also popular malls.

There are lots of places to hang out. The Coffee Bean at KL Plaza has the best collection of trendies in town while, right above it, Tower Records has the best collection of CDs. Coffee Bean is sandwiched by the latest theme restaurant—Planet Hollywood, and the first Starbucks to open in KL. The entire area has been given a make over and the Bintang Walk Project has created a Parisian cafe ambience in the area from Lot 10 to Starhill. Bintang Walk offers gourmet coffee, fine wines and fine dining. This is a great place to see and be seen. Over at Sungei Wang Plaza and Bukit Bintang Plaza, the trendies love to dine at Zang Toi's.

All the big-name hotels are also in this area, including Ritz-Carlton. If you are tired of American fast-food junk and if the hotels' coffeehouses / restaurants are too expensive, check out the hawkers behind Park Royal Hotel or along J. Imbi.

The Rest of KL

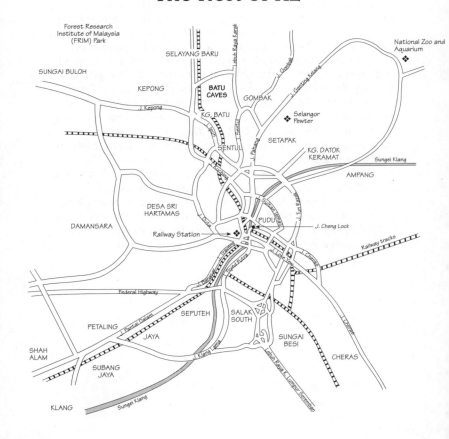

The Iron Bullock Cart

West Towards Klang

*It all started with a speedster
called Lady Clarke...*

Today's railway service from Klang to Kuala Lumpur has been revived with the introduction of the Electric Commuter Service, which has electric trains travelling quickly and quietly through the crowded Klang Valley.

In the old days, the train service was much noisier and slower although at 30 mph, the steam-powered locomotive was probably the fastest and meanest machine then.

When Swettenham took over as Resident in 1882, he studied the possibility of building a road to link Kuala Lumpur to Klang, but the topography of the land was discouraging and he decided to build a railway instead.

However, the credit for the first concrete proposal to build a railway from Kuala Lumpur to Pengkalan Batu (Klang) went not to Swettenham but to a Chinese group backed by a European in Singapore. That group of investors had wanted exclusive rights to transport mail and a monopoly for 15 years on future railway projects.

Barlow says Swettenham was asked to study the proposal and his opinion was that it was better for the railways to be controlled by the government. He also thought the railway line would pay for itself and contribute much to the development of Selangor.

Riding Through Town

In 1892, an extension southwards was built to link the town centre to tin mines in Pudu, spelt 'Pudoh' in the old days. In 1895, it was extended to mines in Sungei Besi. The Pudoh line crossed the Klang river behind the railway station and cut through town crossing Rodger Street and High Street on overhead bridges and went along the middle of Foch Avenue to the Sultan Street station and on to Pudoh. The extra-wide Foch Avenue (now called Jalan Cheng Lock) is a legacy of that railway line.

The Sultan Street station was demolished years ago for road widening.

Surveyors reported in 1883 that 'the preliminary railway survey reveals an almost straight and level line with no engineering difficulties, as yet, appearing'. Construction of the railway was fairly straightforward except for the building of a bridge in Klang and the final costs were $700,000. Work began in late 1883 and by October 1886, the line was complete.

An engineer from the Ceylon Public Work Department, Spence Moss, was put in charge of the construction as he had had some experience as a railway engineer in England before working in Ceylon.

Hill and Rathborne, a major contractor involved in many other ventures in Selangor, provided the railway sleepers, while the ever-reliable Yap Ah Loy provided unskilled workers. Plate laying, which required special skills, was done by Bengalis from India.

Initially, it was a simple railway line without stations, but there was a terminal in Klang—though passengers had to cross the river to reach the terminal—and at the Kuala Lumpur end, there was a temporary terminal in the form of a zinc-roofed shed. Along the route, there were very basic halts at Petaling, Batu Tiga and Bukit Kuda.

Best Bullock Cart

The first locomotive was named Lady Clarke, after the wife of Sir Andrew Clarke, the Governor of the Straits Settlements from 1873 to 1875. The machine had previously been owned by the Maharajah of Johore who had bought it for his grand scheme to run a service on wooden rails from Tanjung Puteri to Gunung Pulai.

Straits Settlements Governor Sir Frederick Weld travelled from Singapore for the opening and after meeting up with Sultan Abdul Samad in Klang, they rode Lady Clarke into Kuala Lumpur. The Sultan said it was the 'best bullock cart' he had travelled in. The trip took 43 minutes.

The whole of Kuala Lumpur gathered to celebrate the event. Some had travelled for hours to witness the grand entrance of the steam-powered monster from which alighted two luminaries—the Sultan and the Governor. It was not very often that Kuala Lumpur hosted such distinguished guests.

Sir Frederick Weld described the scene as 'an exceedingly gay one, bright with costumes and coloured hangings, and banners, and palm and fern leaves'.

When the regular service began, the railways offered four trips between Kuala Lumpur and Klang daily.

In 1889, a bridge was built and the railway line could then be extended to Klang town. The bridge was called Connaught Bridge, named after the Duke and Duchess of Connaught who were visiting Singapore then.

Insider Trading

Judging from old records, insider trading is not a modern phenomenon. It was as common in the British colonial days as it is now.

In 1891, the Resident of Selangor W.E. Maxwell, who was known to have had a frictional relationship with his predecessor Swettenham, had this to say of the land records: 'The result of my investigations was to show that Government Officials of all classes have trafficked largely in land in the State of Selangor and... in many cases, the names of officers' wives, children and other relations crop up on the records.'

However, the Government of that time had no clear-cut policy on such 'investments' and the Colonial Office merely issued instructions prohibiting 'wholesale jobbing in lands' by Government officials. Swettenham himself was implicated in some of these profiteering activities and it was alleged that 'he had extensive investments in land around Klang on the south side of the river' and had ordered the extension of the railway line across Connaught Bridge to boost his investments.

Railway engineer Spence Moss was made the scapegoat in a crackdown on profiteering.

As engineer of the railway, he knew the route of the line and where the extensions would lead to. He bought under his brother-in-law's name 17 lots of land in Klang, five lots in Kuala Lumpur and some in Pudu. Needless to say, these pieces of land were near the railway lines.

After an enquiry was held, Spence Moss was dispensed with.

The railway service was not without incident—the Lady Clarke was badly damaged in a collision with another engine, Lady Clementi, on 11 August 1893, outside Klang. Thirteen people were injured and one of the victims died later. And at least twice, sparks from the engine set fire to seats in the passenger compartment.

The shed in Kuala Lumpur was replaced in 1892 by 'a handsome commodious and well situated building' and in November that year, the Governor Clementi Smith opened the station.

When tin was still an important and profitable commodity, the railway line proved viable after suffering initial losses. In 1890, it carried 6,439 trucks of firewood; 173,796 bags of rice; tin slabs; and 626 chests of opium.

Over the years its role as a commuter service declined with improvements in road connections between Kuala Lumpur and Klang. However, trains continued transporting goods from Kuala Lumpur to Port Swettenham (renamed Port Klang) for export and import purposes.

Some old lines in Kuala Lumpur were left to rot for decades and when the Light Rail Transport system was introduced, several sections were rehabilitated and upgraded for the modern commuter service.

The Klang River 'Highway'

*It is a much faster—and more uneventful—
ride to Klang these days.*

These days, the widened Federal Highway leads from Kuala Lumpur at its junction with Jalan Klang Lama to Klang, passing through the satellite town Petaling Jaya and Shah Alam, the capital of Selangor.

These towns have grown so much that nobody is quite sure where one ends and the other begins. The six-lane highway, which is a toll road, is often jammed during peak hours even though it has been widened. On a good day, the journey will take about half an hour travelling within legal speed limits.

In the old days, the 'highway' was in the form of the Klang river and it took three days to pole upriver all the way to Kuala Lumpur.

According to Haji Abdullah Hukum, it took three days during the rainy season because the river was deeper. During the dry season, it took from 10 to 15 days.

Later, there was a faster way to travel—by taking a steam launch for about four hours along the Klang river to a place called Damansara, about 18 miles from Klang town, which was as far as launches could travel back then.

Passengers had to disembark there and use a track to go to Kuala Lumpur 17 miles away. They could either walk or ride on ponies and the journey took another four hours.

From Damansara, the track went north to a point called Batu Tiga (which was named thus because it was three miles from Damansara) and then east towards Kuala Lumpur, reaching the town by way of Penchala and what later became Bluff Road (now called Jalan Bukit Aman).

American naturalist William T. Hornaday, who visited Selangor and Kuala Lumpur from June to July 1878, described the track as 'a good carriage road'.

He wrote in his book *Two Years In The Jungle*: 'The road lay through very dense, high forest, composed of large and very lofty trees (among which the camphor was often noticed), growing

" A good carriage road. "

very thickly together, while the ground underneath was choked with an undergrowth of thorny palms, rattans and brush so thick it seemed that nothing larger than a cat could get through it. Nowhere was there the smallest opening in this dark and damp mass of vegetation, and it made me shudder to think of attempting to go through it. Surely, I thought, we will not attempt to hunt in such a forest as that.'

Eight miles from Damansara, the good carriage road ended and to reach Kuala Lumpur, his party had to travel on a 'very rough bridle path through hilly jungle and across many muddy little streams'.

At the 12th mile, he passed the Sungei Batu police station and after passing two or three clearings, he reached the top of a long, steep hill and at the foot lay Kuala Lumpur lying on the opposite side of the Klang river.

'A sampan came across to ferry us over, while our ponies swam beside it,' Hornaday wrote.

It was quite an adventure to travel from Klang to KL those days. Nowadays, the only adventure would be avoiding speed traps.

Stinking Discovery

Jalan Batu Caves
Off Jalan Ipoh

Of skulls and skeletons, five-legged
bulls, and the demon Asura...

Batu caves

Was it the smell of durian or guano that led American naturalist William T. Hornaday to the Batu Caves? Indeed, there was a 'very curious pungent odor (sic)' that was carried by the wind from the caves to Hornaday's hunting party, which included Syers, the police chief.

Covering the floors of the caves were thick layers of guano collected over the centuries, but growing in the vicinity were numerous durian trees with ripening fruit.

Hornaday and company were guided to the limestone outcrop by an elderly Malay and several Jakuns (spelt 'Jacoons' by Hornaday) and when they stepped into a cathedral-like cave, Hornaday was so awestruck by the size and beauty of the chamber that he sang three notes—Sol, Mi, Do. The notes reverberated in the massive chamber and the echoes were sweet, haunting and inspiring.

Syers was less musical and much more plebeian in his method—he fired a shot from his gun and the echo sounded like 'a deep boom of thunder'.

Hornaday, the American naturalist has been credited with discovering Batu Caves, which back in 1878, was in the middle of the jungle. His account of his so-called discovery is contained in his book *Two Years In the Jungle* and answers the question of who was the first to discover Batu Caves. The officer in charge of Lands, Surveys and Public Works, D.D. Daly, had also written an account in which he implies that he was the one who discovered the caves.

Hornaday was the chief taxidermist of the US National Museum and visited Singapore and Selangor from June to July 1878.

However there is some dispute over the credit for the discovery because several caves in the limestone hill already had Malay names such as Gua Belah, Gua Lada and Gua Lambong which suggest that the local Malays had already known of their existence. Furthermore, the aborigines—the Jakuns—had traditionally been using the caves as shelter from wild elephants and other dangerous animals. They had also been catching bats in the caves.

Nevertheless, his account of his trip makes good reading. From Kuala Lumpur, he and Syers travelled on ponies through the jungle for six miles to Batu.

The Five-Legged Bull

Beside the road leading to the 272-step staircase at Batu Caves, there is a statue of a bull with five legs—the fifth sprouting from somewhere close to the spine near the neck. At the base, there is a plaque with the words: 'Died 8/2/72. Erected 7/1/73 in memory of our temple Nandhi whose contribution to the temple has become a legend.'

The first thought in the mind of the visitor would be: 'What was that all about?'

The story of the bull with five legs which attained a holy significance to Hindus, began in 1957 when it was born in Banting, Selangor.

Its owner, sensing that it was something special, donated it to the Batu Caves temple, where it roamed for 15 years. The entire compound at the base of the temple was its home, especially the football field. It could do whatever it liked, and it kept the grass short by munching it.

It became a celebrity and tourists from near and far started turning up to photograph it. The bull contributed to the fame of Batu Caves throughout the world.

Apparently, it was also a sensitive animal and it could not bear to see its kind being ill-treated and would get very angry whenever it saw a fellow bull being used as a beast of burden and punished by its human owner.

In its old age, it fought with a younger bull. After two fights, its horns were badly damaged and after being sick for 40 days, it died.

The five-legged bull was buried at the foot of the Batu Caves and devotees erected the statue in memory of it.

Pungent Odour

Hornaday described the jungle around Batu as swampy in places, but so open that one could go through it on foot with tolerable ease. 'Here and there were patches of low and thin forest, broken occasionally with fine grassy glades.'

He came across a 'tree-house of the Jacoons (sic)' and found out that they were in the area to capture bats from a nearby cave. The Jakuns acted as their guide and took them hunting.

When they returned from one of the hunting trips, they noticed a peculiar smell in the air. 'We noticed in the air a very curious, pungent odor, like guano, the cause of which we could not divine.' Syers asked an old Malay man who was with the party where the smell came from and the reply was that it was bat's dung from a nearby cave.

'We turned about directly and made for the cliff, under the old man's guidance. The cave was soon reached. We climbed up 40 feet (12 metres) or so over a huge pile of angular rocks that had fallen from the face of the cliff, and on going down a sharp incline found ourselves underneath a huge mass of bare limestone rock, leaning at an angle of 45 degrees against the side of the cliff, forming a cavernous arch, open at both ends and a hundred feet high. It was hung with smooth, dull-grey stalactites, which, when broken off, showed such a clean white limestone formation that might almost be called marble'.

'From near the bottom of this curiously formed arch a wide opening led into the cave proper. We procured a torch of dry bamboo and entered forthwith. This cave... it seems is called Gua Belah, or the Double Cave... The floor was covered to an unknown depth with a layer of loose and dry guano.'

For the next few days, they explored the limestone outcrop and its various caves such as Gua Lada and Gua Lambong.

Skulls and Skeletons

On 2 January 1955, two British explorers—John Harnden, 27, and Tom Hungerfrod, 28—who were working with Sime Darby and Company, went cave-climbing and found a skeleton in a crevice in the Dark Caves.

On the wall of the cave was a message in Mandarin: 'If anybody else should come to this spot, he should sign his name. I am a Cantonese from Lok Wooi district in South China. I was born in Lung Sow Poh village. My name is Chan Kai San. 3 February in the 28th year of the Chinese Republic (1940)'. Six days later, the skeleton was removed. Chan was believed to have committed suicide.

The two explorers did not sign their names because they could not read the Chinese script and the message was translated when they returned to Kuala Lumpur. Five months later, the same two explorers went to the Dark Caves and discovered four more skeletons in another crevice near the first find.

The skeletons most likely were those of communist terrorists who had used the caves to hide from British and Malayan soldiers during the Emergency.

'At the mouth (of Gua Lambong) there is a perfect little vestibule scooped out of the solid rock by the hand of nature for the express accommodation of the party who will keep a stand there for the sale of refreshments, photographs and torches to the tourists who will visit the cave during the next century.' Hornaday foresaw the touristic potential of Batu Caves, but he never expected it to be a place of worship.

It was at Gua Lambong that they discovered the cave which was to be the site of the Hindu shrine found there today.

'We found ourselves in a grand cathedral. We walked along a grand gallery with clean and level floor, perpendicular walls and gothic roof, like the nave of a cathedral, 50 feet (15.2 metres) wide and 60 feet (18.3 metres) high.'

'A grand cathedral ...'

'At the far end, the roof rose in a great round dome 90 or 100 feet high perfectly resembling St. Peter's in Rome.' The Batu Caves did become a place of worship, but the pilgrims were not Christians.

Abode of Murugan

The Indians who ventured to Malaya for work were mostly Tamils and they were Hindus who worshipped Siva and Murugan. Another deity, who was worshipped by the Indian community as their protector in this foreign land, was Mariamman.

In Hinduism, Murugan's temples are always located on hilltops simply because, in the religion's mythology, Murugan flew to a hill and refused to descend after he was outwitted by his brother Vinayagar in a contest in which the prize was a golden apple belonging to another deity, Narada. Thus devotees had to climb hills or mountains to reach their god.

A temple for Mariamman was built at High Street (now called Jalan Tun H. S. Lee) by Thamboosamy Pillai, the richest Indian around at that time. And when he asked Theiravangadom Pillay and Kanthappa Thaver to find a place for Murugan's temple, they looked no further than Batu Caves.

The Sri Subramania Swamy Temple was set up at Batu Caves in 1891 and from the following year onwards Thaipusam was, and still is, celebrated there annually.

In the old days, pilgrims had to undergo the risky and strenuous task of climbing the almost vertical rocky face of Batu Caves to reach the temple 61 metres above the base. A rickety wooden staircase was built circa 1920 and it was only in 1940 that the famed 272-step concrete staircase was built at a cost of $50,000.

A funicular railway was built in 1973 and, 10 years later, the problem-ridden service stopped operating.

Gallery of Gods

At the base of the limestone, there are two smaller caves which have been turned into art galleries. These galleries were the earliest projects of the Batu Caves Development Committee, formed in 1971 to promote tourism.

Sculptors from India were commissioned to produce various Hindu deities for the first gallery, which was opened on 7 January 1973.

The adjoining cave, which has a large bat and pigeon population, was turned into the Valluvar Kottam (Valluvar's Gallery). Opened on 27 January 1980, it features about a third of the poetry of the Indian-Hindu saint Thiruvalluvar, who wrote 1,330 poems, comprising two-line couplets. These are now considered masterpieces of Tamil poetry.

Statues and wall-paintings, depicting scenes from these poems, line the walls. Carved in Tamil script on white marble slabs, each poem contains about 10 verses.

Taking centrestage in this cave is a black granite bust of the poet, which was carved in India.

All's Vel at Batu Caves

At the beginning of every year, almost a million Hindu Indians and tourists will be at Batu Caves to witness one of the goriest,

A Hindu devotee during the colourful festival of Thaipusam.

noisiest and most colourful festivals celebrated in Malaysia.

This is Thaipusam, which is celebrated during Thai, the 10th month of the Hindu calendar, when the full moon passes through a *nakshatra* (lunar station) called Pusam.

This is the day that Murugan is believed to have received the Vel, the Invincible Spear, from his mother Parvati. Murugan used the Vel to conquer evil. In South India, it coincides with the harvesting season and according to astrology, it is a time of good fortune. In the Western calendar, it normally falls in late January or early February.

Good Over Evil

The demon Asura was killed by Murugan's Vel and the story goes that when hit by the spear, Asura split into two, one part becoming a peacock and the other a crow. Thus *kavadis* feature crow shapes and peacock feathers which symbolise the conquest of good over evil.

At Batu Caves itself, scores of *kavadi* carriers will be at the gateway waiting for their turn to dance to drumbeats along the sea of humanity, climb the stairs and pay homage to Murugan.

The *kavadi* carriers would have the spear-like skewers and hooks pierced into their bodies, and through cheeks and tongues by priests at another spot beside a stream a few hundred metres from the gateway. To prepare for *kavadi*-carrying, the penitent must abstain from worldly things, such as sex, for a month and eat vegetarian food while offering regular prayers. In return, Murugan may answer his or her requests.

The *kavadi* is a tray with an arch over it which symbolises a chariot, signifying that the devotee is carrying the deity on his or her shoulders to perform the penance. On the tray are offerings of a bowl of milk, flowers, fruit and rock sugar. On the structure are peacock feathers, crow symbols and images of Murugan.

There are other methods of penitence—some women carry urns of milk up the stairs while children simply have their heads shaven. There are macabre ways as well— cutting of tongues or slashing of bodies. Over the years, the skewers became longer and longer and a limit of one metre was imposed, out of consideration for other pilgrims.

In the cave-temple, priests remove the hooks, spears, and skewers and smear ash over the wounds to prevent bleeding.

This annual celebration was almost brought to an end in January 1993 when a *yogi* sought a court order to stop the Thaipusam festival until the Batu Caves was consecrated otherwise evil spirits would possess the pilgrims.

His argument was that the 63-year-old chief priest had died before the consecration ceremony to cleanse the caves was due to be completed a month before.

The temple management committee argued that the chief priest had completed the morning session of the consecration ceremony and then had a heart attack during the lunch break and died on the way to the hospital, but the ritual had been completed by other priests in the evening. The High Court in Shah Alam ruled against the *yogi* and the festival was held without any supernatural incident other than the usual number of people entering trances and the *kavadi* carriers having their tongues and cheeks pierced without bleeding.

Kuala Lumpur itself will be all jammed up as roads are closed for the procession of the Silver Chariot bearing the statuettes of Murugan and his consorts, Valli and Teivayanni, from the Sri Maha Mariamman Temple at Jalan Tun H.S. Lee to Batu Caves. When the festival ends, the roads are jammed again for the return journey.

Two white bullocks will pull the chariot and crowds of devotees, lining the streets, will smash coconuts to cleanse the path for the deity. There will be shouts of 'Vel, Vel, Vetri Vel!' which can be translated as 'The Spear, The Spear, The Invincible Spear!'

Greenies in the Caves

The Batu Caves was gazetted as a reserve for public recreation in 1930 but in the 1950s, permission was somehow given to two quarry operators to blast the limestone hill to make building materials.

Blasting with sticks of dynamite was conducted for many years and several caves like the Sakai Cave and Quarry Cave were destroyed. The bat population in the other caves was also affected. People living in the vicinity were disturbed by the clouds of dust stirred up by the blasts—many came down with breathing problems, sore throats, sinus and bronchitis. Asthmatic patients in particular suffered very badly. Yet everyone endured in silence.

It was only in the late 70s that the environmentalists started fighting back against Government and the big businesses. Politicians and the media joined in the fray.

After a prolonged campaign, the environmentalists won. Blasting was stopped in January 1981 though the quarries continued grinding their stockpiles of limestone boulders for some time.

Meanwhile, at the Dark Caves—a system of caves that extends into the deep interior of the limestone hill, accessible by an entrance beside the staircase just below the Temple Cave—the public and adventurers were damaging the fragile ecosystem.

In December 1987, the authorities decided to close the Dark Caves to the public and only researchers could gain access to them. Over the years, the life forms in the caves such as bats, cockroaches, beetles, moths, centipedes, mole-crickets and snakes have been rejuvenated.

Baldie and the Bentong Kid

Around KL

*A misguided genius and a sadistic sociopath
on a rampage of crime in KL...*

Kuala Lumpur is a peaceful place. Though not exactly crime-free, it is relatively safe compared to other cities. One can walk in the main streets of the city late at night and still return home unscathed.

But the city has had its share of career criminals.

The first was a self-styled Robin Hood who held the belief that he could do his bit to change society by robbing the rich to help the poor.

Though the police vehemently denied the 'good' deeds of Botak (Malay for 'bald') Chin, there were no lack of stories about poor old men and women living in the squatter settlements of Kuala Lumpur, waking up to find wads of money or boxes of provisions in their homes. Even today, years after Botak Chin was executed **A folk hero ...** at the gallows on 11 June 1981, he still remains something like a folk hero. And quite frequently those who remember leave flowers or cigarettes at the urn containing his ashes at the Chin Fatt Sze Temple at the Jalan Kerayung cemetery.

Botak Chin wanted to lord over the KL underworld and if imitation is the greatest form of flattery, then Botak Chin must have been flattered—it was rumoured that some other crooks claimed to be Botak Chin when committing robberies.

Botak Chin was born in Kuala Lumpur on 3 March 1951 to a family of modest means—his father worked in the Malayan Railways. His name on his birth certificate was Wong See Chin and he was the fifth of 10 children.

He studied at Chung Mun (Chinese) primary school at Sentul Pasar and spent a year in Form One at the nearby Methodist Boys' School. He dropped out of school, not because he was stupid (indeed a leading psychiatrist called him a misguided genius) but from lack of money.

To supplement his family's income, he found a job at the Maxwell Road (now called Jalan Mahameru) wholesale market (which has since shifted to Selayang) as a vegetable stall worker earning $40 a month. He stayed with his family at the Sentul Railway quarters.

Later, he spent some time working with his father at the Railway workshop but he quit after a short stint.

At the wholesale market, he met 360 Gang members who controlled much of Sentul. Bullied by them, he picked up some martial arts skills for his own defence but later joined the gang.

Guns and Grenades

Near his house, there were some robbers who were in his circle of friends. Fired up by their tales of derring-do, riches to be made and lavish lifestyles, he decided that robbing was better than selling vegetables.

In 1969, he met up with Ah Yip Chat, a bad hat who had escaped from police custody. He was then introduced to another criminal, Tor Tee.

The trio staged their first robbery on 17 April 1969 at Batu Lima Village in Jinjang.

With his share of the spoils, he bought a gun. Botak Chin had a certain fascination for guns and with the increasing frequency and daring of his robberies, his collection of firearms increased in tandem.

Towards the end of his criminal career, **A fascination** his gang had burgeoned to 12 members and **for guns ...** they had 25 guns and five hand grenades.

After the successful first robbery, he met an old friend called Ah Kong Chai who was roped into his gang. The foursome committed eight robberies before police nabbed Botak Chin on 16 October 1969 and he was given a 12-year jail term. On appeal, the sentence was reduced to seven years' jail. In November 1974, he was released from the Taiping prison.

At that point in life, Botak Chin could have considered turning over a new leaf selling vegetables at the wholesale market. In fact, he did work there again at a higher pay of $120 a month.

But something lured him back to his old ways—it could have been the influence of his old gangster cronies or he could have missed the thrill of it all. He resisted temptation, or fate, for a while but his resolve dissolved and Robin Hood rode again.

In May 1975, he formed a four-man gang with some 360 Gang members. They were Ng Chang Wong alias Ah Wong, who was killed by Botak Chin on 29 November 1975; Teh Bock Loy alias Seng Chai, who shot himself rather than surrender when trapped by police on 9 December 1975; and Bah Kok Chin alias Pangkor Chai, who was shot dead by police on 16 February 1976 during a police raid which resulted in the capture of Botak Chin himself.

At Padang Besar, he bought guns—a .32 Walther automatic for himself, a .22 revolver for Ah Wong and a King Cobra for Pangkor Chai.

With the new gang, he started his reign as King of Crime on 2 February 1975, hitting a gambling den in Setapak and escaping with RM5,800.

Self-Styled Robin Hood

The gang committed at least 28 robberies with loot amounting to about half a million ringgit, which they spent on high living in Kuala Lumpur, Thailand and Hong Kong. At least a portion of the loot went to 'charity'—penniless squatters, needy old folks and families whose members had been killed or arrested.

Botak Chin was an enigma. He was a criminal; yet he looked upon himself as some kind of do-gooder. He sympathised with the poor and downtrodden, perhaps because he came from an impoverished background and could identify with them; yet he was a cold-blooded killer who murdered his own friends such as Ah Wong and Tua Pui Lek, leader of the Jinjang-based Ng Chee San gang, whose bullet-riddled bodies were found in a tin mining area in Segambut. Ah Wong was killed, apparently, because he was losing control of the gang and Tua Pui Lek for failing to deliver some guns.

He was also an unpredictable character. When Prime Minister Tun Razak died, Botak Chin sent his family a wreath.

Not Brave, But Foolish

Botak Chin's story unfolds like a Hong Kong TV serial. Even after being caught by police and sentenced to death by the High Court, the drama of Botak Chin did not reach its final episode.

A lawyer, Jagjit Singh, fought a five-year legal battle to set him free.

Botak Chin was the first man to plead guilty under the Internal Security Act at the High Court on 11 January 1977. He had turned down the court's offer to give him time to think it over before making a decision. He also thanked Jagjit Singh and S.T. Lee for agreeing to defend him.

The judge called him a brave and honest man and Botak Chin replied that he was not brave, but foolish. Whether the judge agreed with him or not was immaterial, he was sentenced to death.

Later, he agreed to appeal and his appeal to the Federal Court was dismissed in April 1977. The case went up to the Privy Council and on 24 January 1979, the Privy Council ruled that the conviction be quashed and the death sentence set aside.

A new trial took place and this time he pleaded not guilty. But he was found guilty and again sentenced to death. An appeal to the Federal Court was dismissed on 23 September 1980. A last-hope appeal to the Pardons Board was rejected. And that, was the last episode.

He also had certain codes of behaviour for his gang members—they had to sport crew cuts and were banned from using drugs. They also always rode on Yamaha motorcycles.

During a robbery at Sentul Railway Club, near his house, he put two guns on the table and challenged his victims to draw cowboy-style. That could have been due to the influence of Westerns on television.

He even tried to kill his nemesis, the top cop Deputy Superintendent of Police S. Kulasingam who was tracking him down. In November 1975 while Kulasingam was cruising around the Jalan Imbi area looking for Botak Chin (whom an informer said was in the vicinity), the hunter became the hunted as Botak Chin trailed him in a car, overtook the cop and shot him twice. Kulasingam managed to drive to the Cheras police station for help.

The hunter became the hunted ...

Kulasingam survived, but Botak Chin did not. By then, the entire police force in the city was out for his blood. At 8.45 pm on 16 February 1976, Botak Chin and his gang were hiding in a sawmill at Jalan Ipoh when police surrounded it and ambushed them. The crooks fought back, but they were out-gunned and outnumbered. Two gang members were killed in the fight and Botak Chin, and two others, arrested.

Botak Chin was sentenced to death by the High Court but even in prison, there was drama.

While on death row, he grappled with his warders in a vain escape attempt, stabbing three of them, on 1 January 1981.

But the drama had to end and Botak Chin had his last meal of Kentucky Fried Chicken, fried mee, fruits and water. Then he was a 'dead man walking' and the noose of the hangman's rope cut into his skin... Before he was hung in prison at 3 am on 11 June 1981, he offered to donate his eyes and kidneys for transplants, but the offer was rejected.

From Small Town to Big City

The second crook did not receive such veneration and the public were indeed very relieved and happy that he was shot to death by police in an early morning raid.

Bentong Kali, nicknamed after the Pahang small town he was born in, was probably more cold-blooded than Botak Chin. He was also more trigger-happy, shooting a total stranger for no other reason than for having scolded him for urinating near the victim's flat.

Bentong Kali was into drugs—he wanted to be the Drug Lord, the chief pusher in town and his gun did the talking for him.

Bentong Kali, 32, was shot dead at 6.30 am on 29 June 1993, in a double-storeyed link house located at a dead-end road in the middle-class area of Medan Damansara. Barely an hour earlier, he had shot his 17th victim, a *teh tarik* stall owner.

Killed with him were henchmen S. Gunalan, 31, alias Billiard, and T Gunasegaran alias Raub Guna, 32. Raub is another small town in Pahang.

Thus ended his reign of terror in a hail of bullets from the Special Action Squad. And true to form, Bentong Kali died clutching a German-made Sig Sauer automatic pistol.

Bentong Kali was the kind of crook who lived violently and died violently. **A violent life ...**

Even after his death there was violence.

Two press photographers, assigned to the General Hospital mortuary to cover his family and relatives taking out the body for burial, were assaulted by a group of men.

The police base at the hospital then received an anonymous call that Bentong Kali's men were going to attack the mortuary and police had to send in several truckloads of riot squad police.

When he was buried in his hometown, police recorded the event on video. There were lots of cops around just in case emotions got the better of the mourners.

Bentong Kali was born on 22 January 1961, and he was named after his grandfather who was, in turn, named after the Hindu goddess of destruction, Kaliamma.

When he was barely 14, he dropped out of school and felt there was a better future with a Chinese-led gang in Bentong called 04. He was jailed at 19, a year after his marriage.

Released in March 1980, he moved to the Malaysian Big Apple—Kuala Lumpur—where the lights were bright and there was plenty of money for the picking.

Born to Die

He worked in a market, a coffeeshop and bakery before joining the 08 Indian gang in 1984 which controlled Brickfields, Segambut, Sungei Way and Ampang. He also worked as a car repossessor.

Bentong Kali was in and out of prison so often and had so many brushes with the law that his file must have been very thick.

He was arrested on July 1985 and sent to Pulau Jerejak. Released in 1987, he was sent to Kuantan as a restricted resident for a year.

He returned to Kuala Lumpur and worked as a house detective for a department store at Jalan Klang Lama. In 1989, he formed his own 04 gang in the Jalan Kelang Lama area distributing heroin.

In April 1990, he was arrested in a drug raid and sent to a restricted residence in Gopeng, Perak, for two years.

In November 1991, he escaped from the lawmen whilst attending a court case in Petaling Jaya. After that, he decided to go big time. After picking up some guns, he started his trigger-happy reign, muscling his way around. When district drug or crime lords did not want to cooperate with him, he simply removed the opposition by killing them.

A Shrink Sums Up

The two crooks who terrorised Kuala Lumpur and left indelible marks in the minds of its residents were described as a 'misguided genius' and a 'sadistic sociopath' by a leading psychiatrist.

Datuk Seri Dr M Mahadevan, former director of Hospital Bahagia, a mental hospital in Tanjung Rambutan, Perak, was reported as opining that Bentong Kali was 'emotional, dramatic and erratic' and was 'an incorrigible character with no conscience and never accepts blame or remorse for his actions'. Bentong Kali suffered from marked paranoia and sadistic traits.

'Unlike Botak Chin who was a misguided and distorted genius, Bentong Kali is a homicidal and sadistic sociopath. Botak Chin was a misguided, self-styled idealist with grandiose ideas from young and wanted to be popular. He was more of a socialist.'

A workshop owner was found charred in a burnt car in Kampung Segambut in August 1992. On 24 January 1992, a printing press proprietor was shot while having supper. And that was just the beginning.

In November 1992, police offered a RM10,000 reward for information leading to his arrest. This increased to RM100,000 as the tally of murders went up.

During the hunt for him, Bentong Kali had the audacity to telephone CID Director Zaman Khan and dare Zaman to arrest him. However, unlike Botak Chin, Bentong Kali did not go so far as to attempt to kill the top cop.

It is not certain when he decided to tattoo his body, but the tattoos helped police in the positive identification of his body after his final shoot-out. On his body were tattoos of a dragon, tiger and nude women and on his right arm were the words, Born To Dai (sic).

Li Choi's Reign

In 1894, there were 'robberies of European houses, Government offices and other places almost of nightly occurrence, and the whole neighbourhood was simply in the hands of a well-organised gang who carried on their depredations with impunity'.

This was the reign of Li Choi, the chief crook in the Kuala Lumpur of the 1890s. This man, who was believed to have murdered nine people, had his nemesis in the form of police chief Syers who brought his reign to a welcome end.

But catching the thug was not so simple. Only after much hard work did Syers manage to infiltrate his gang and obtain information on his movements and plans for heists. In a raid, Syers nabbed the gang members, but Li Choi gave him the slip.

Syers had to place detachments of plain clothes constables and detectives in various places and increase the number of night patrols. The cat and mouse game ended with Li Choi's capture in 1895.

During the trial, Li Choi admitted that the spoils of his nefarious deeds included at least three heavy iron Government safes. Li Choi was later executed.

A CLOSER LOOK ...

At the rest of KL—work out your hangover by conquering the steps at Batu Caves. A short drive from the city centre, Batu Caves offers a most unique sight. How often do you get to see a hilltop Hindu temple with the shrines built in a huge cave? If you have time to visit only one tourist spot, Batu Caves is the best bet.

At the edge of the city in the vicinity of Kepong, there is a spot for nature-lovers. Called the Forest Research Institute of Malaysia (FRIM) Park, it is a large tract of virgin jungle hemmed in by housing and industrial estates. I sometimes go there with my family for picnics and a cool, refreshing dip in the jungle stream. It's a pleasant place where you can get away from the 'concreteness' and grime of the city.

Bangsar's success as a trendy entertainment spot has given rise to at least two copycat developments. One is in the Taman Desa / Danau Desa area, off J. Klang Lama, and the other is in the Desa Sri Hartamas area. Recently, the Desa Sri Hartamas nightspot has become 'happening' and KL's 'nightbirds' are flocking there.

Bibliography

Books

Adnan Haji Nawang. *Kuala Lumpur dari Perspektif Haji Adbullah Hukum.* Malaysia: Berita Publishing Sdn Bhd, 1997.

Barlow, H. S. *Swettenham.* Malaysia: Southdene Sdn Bhd, 1995.

Bird, Isabella. *The Golden Chersonese.* London: John Murray, 1883. (Reprinted by Oxford University Press in 1993 in Malaysia)

Guide to Kuala Lumpur's Notable Buildings. Malaysia: The Malaysian Institute of Architects (PAM), 1976.

Gullick, J. M. *Kuala Lumpur 1880 - 1895, A City in the Making.* Malaysia: Pelanduk Publications Sdn Bhd, 1988.

Gullick, J. M. *The Story of Kuala Lumpur, 1857 - 1939.* Malaysia: Eastern Universities Press Sdn Bhd, 1983.

Hornaday, William T. *Two Years in the Jungle.* London: Kegan Paul, Trench & Trubner, 1885.

Professor Datuk Khoo Kay Kim. *Kuala Lumpur—The Formative Years.* Malaysia: Berita Publishing Sdn Bhd, 1996.

Middlebrook, S. M., and J. M. Gullick. *Yap Ah Loy.* Malaysia: The Malaysian Branch of the Royal Asiatic Society, 1983. (Previously published as The Journal of the Malayan Branch of the Royal Asiatic Society Volume XXIV Part 2, July 1951. Republished as The Malaysian Branch of the Royal Asiatic Society Reprint No. 9, June 1983.)

Swettenham, Frank. *Malay Sketches.* UK: Bodley Head Ltd, 1895. (Reprinted by Graham Brash (Pte) Ltd in 1984 in Singapore.)

Yeang, Ken. *The Architecture of Malaysia.* Malaysia: Pepin Press, 1992.

Articles

Tunku Ismail Jewa. "Life of the Tunku at the Residency." New Straits Times article on 7/9/1992.

Nair, Prabhakaran and Liang Poh Chu. "Signposts of History." *New Straits Times Annual 1992.* Malaysia: New Straits Times Press (M) Bhd, 1992.

Sheppard, Tan Sri Dr Mubin. "The Home that Frank Built." *New Straits Times Annual 1993.* Malaysia: New Straits Times Press (M) Bhd, 1993.

About the Author

Ever since leaving secondary school in 1976, Lam Seng Fatt has spent most of his time in journalism. At the tender and innocent age of 18, he joined *New Straits Times* as a crime reporter. Over the years, he covered almost every field from entertainment to politics. Along the way, he picked up photography and became a photojournalist and travel writer.

He also reviewed music and books and held a few exhibitions of his photographic works at private galleries and the National Art Gallery. In 1991, he left the *New Straits Times* to try commodities trading. Eighteen months later, he decided that palm oil was not his cup of tea and rejoined *New Straits Times* and worked on directories and magazines, including the *New Straits Times Annual*.

His first book, *Through The Lens*, on photography was published in 1996. In June 1999, he left *New Straits Times* and joined *The Star* as an assistant editor.

Index